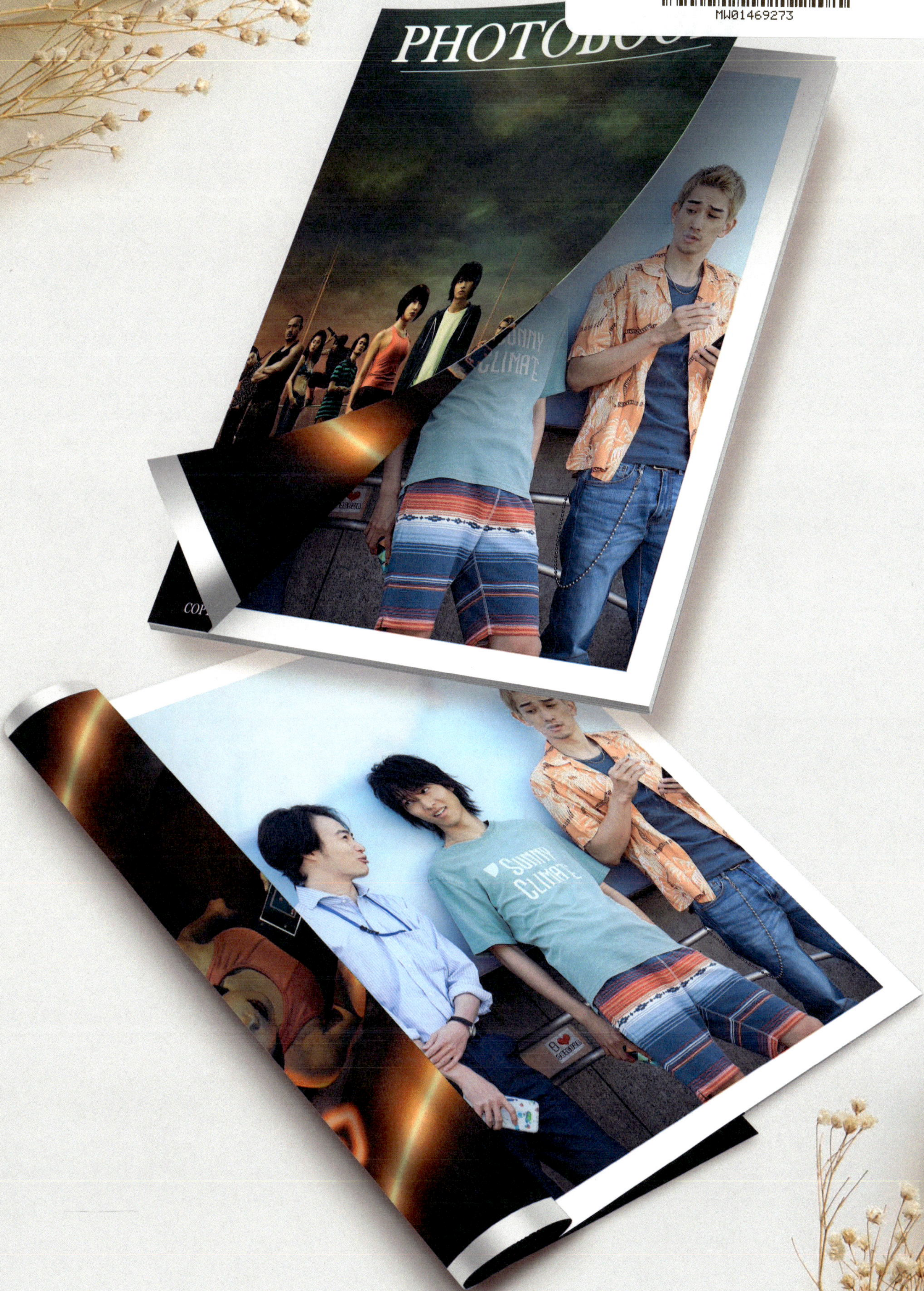
SUNNY CLIMATE

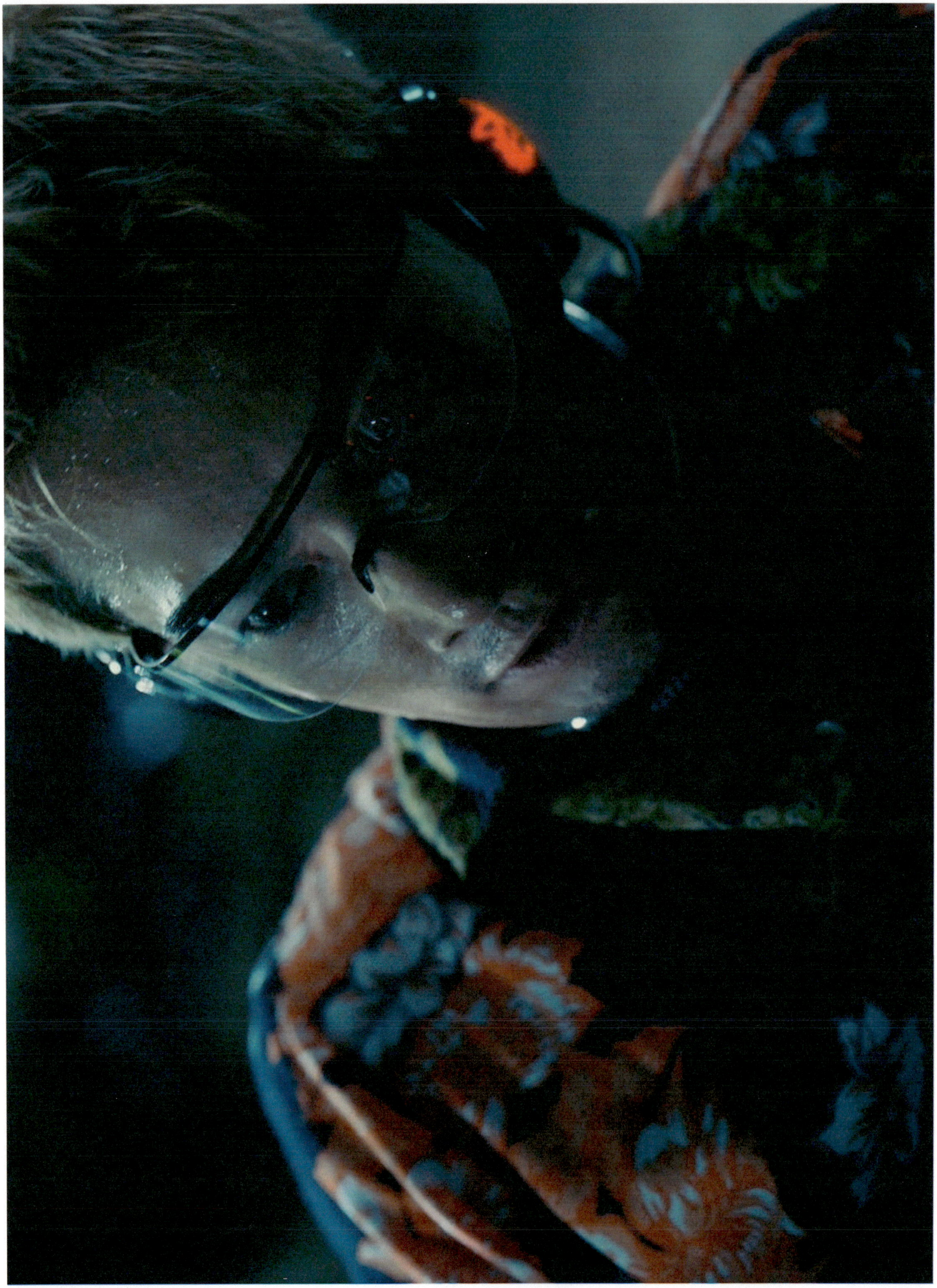

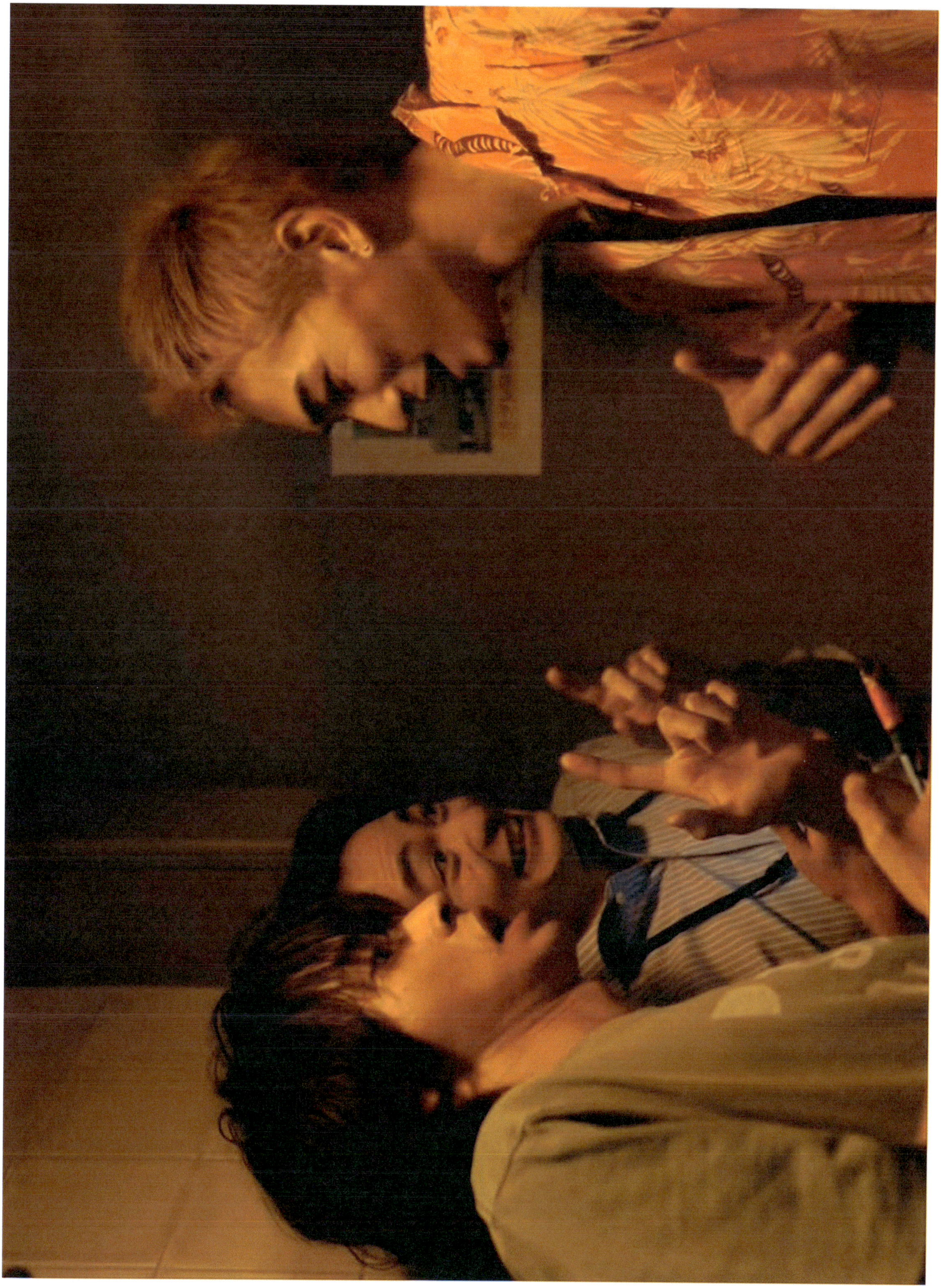

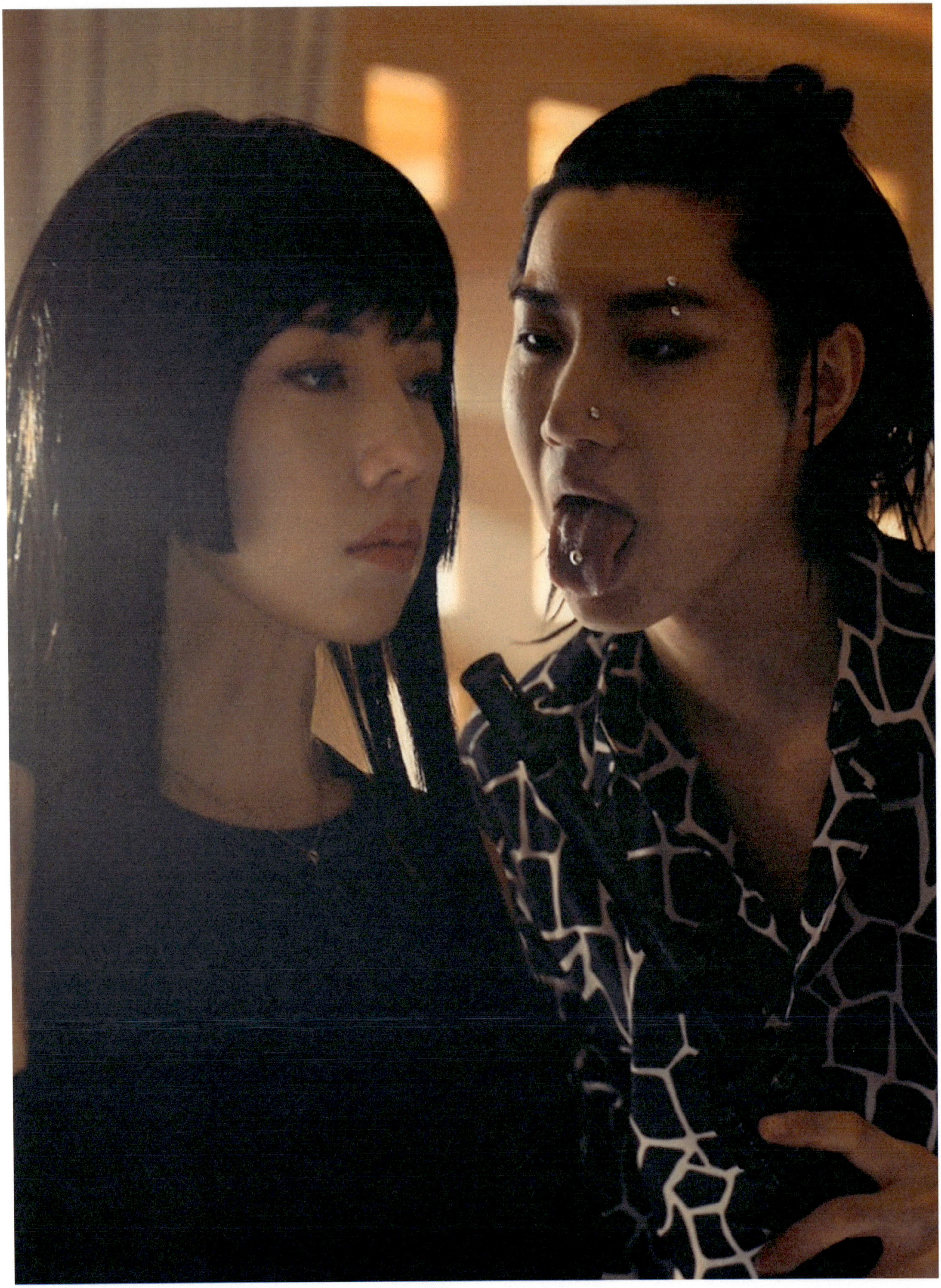

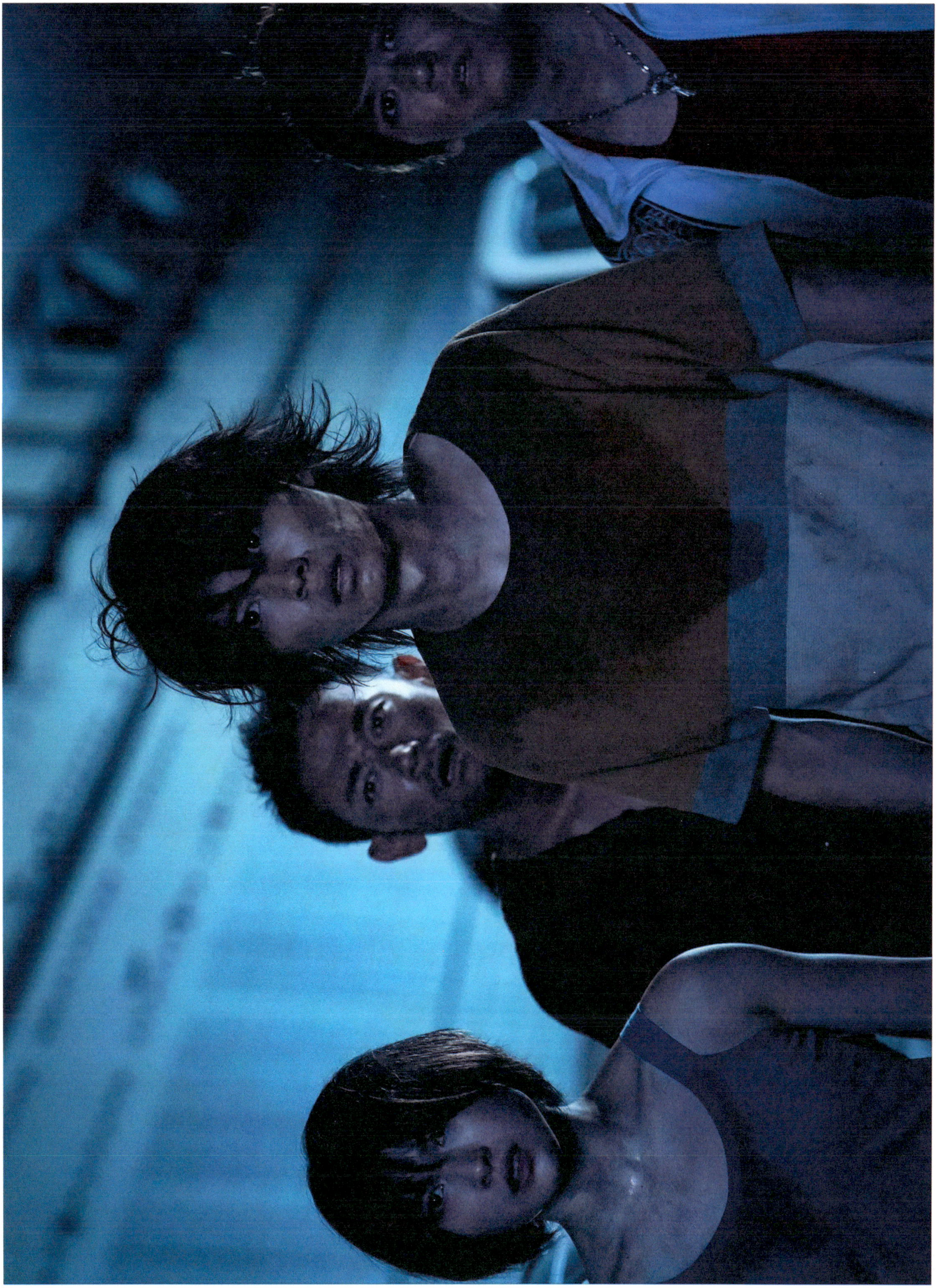

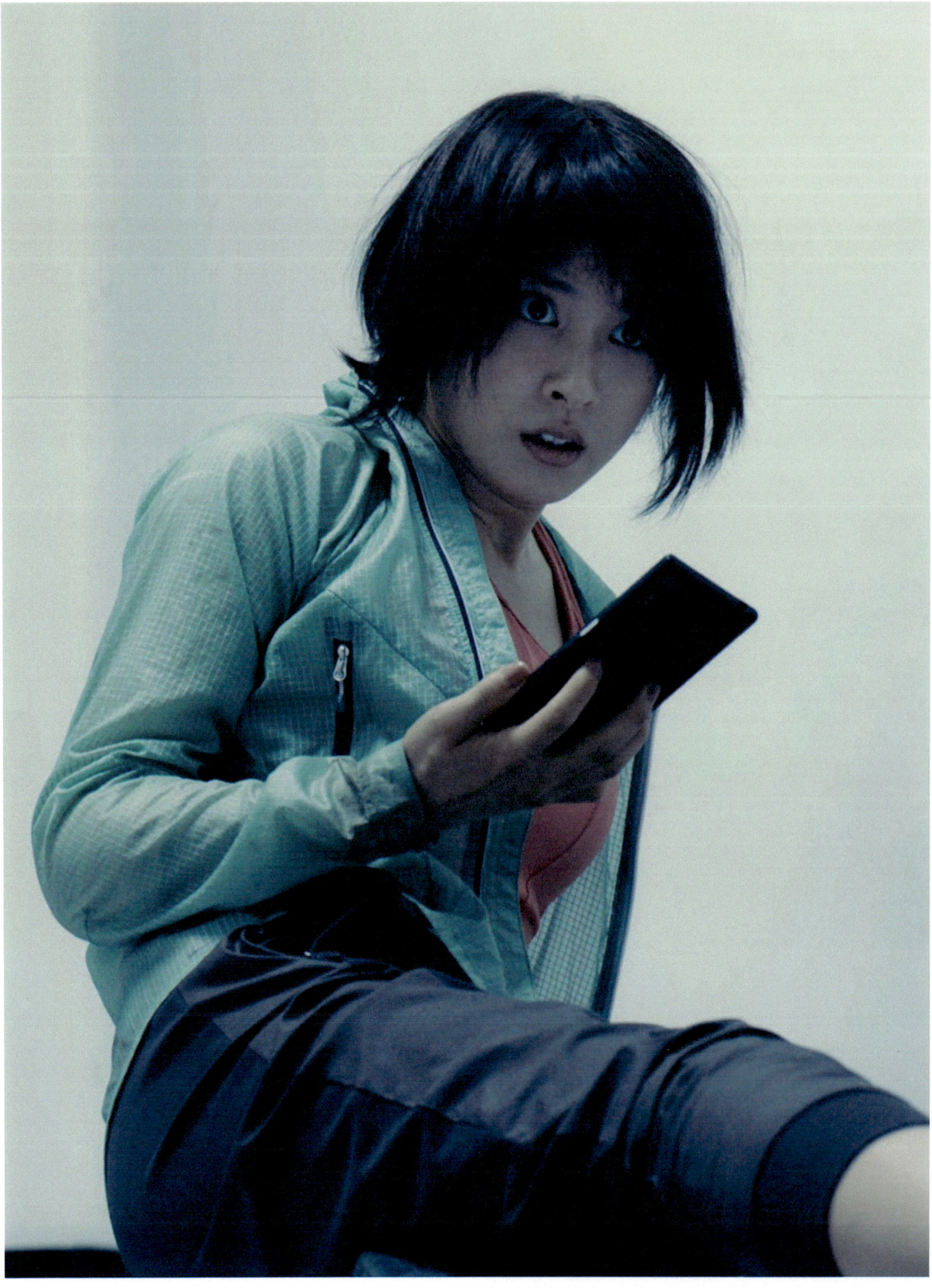

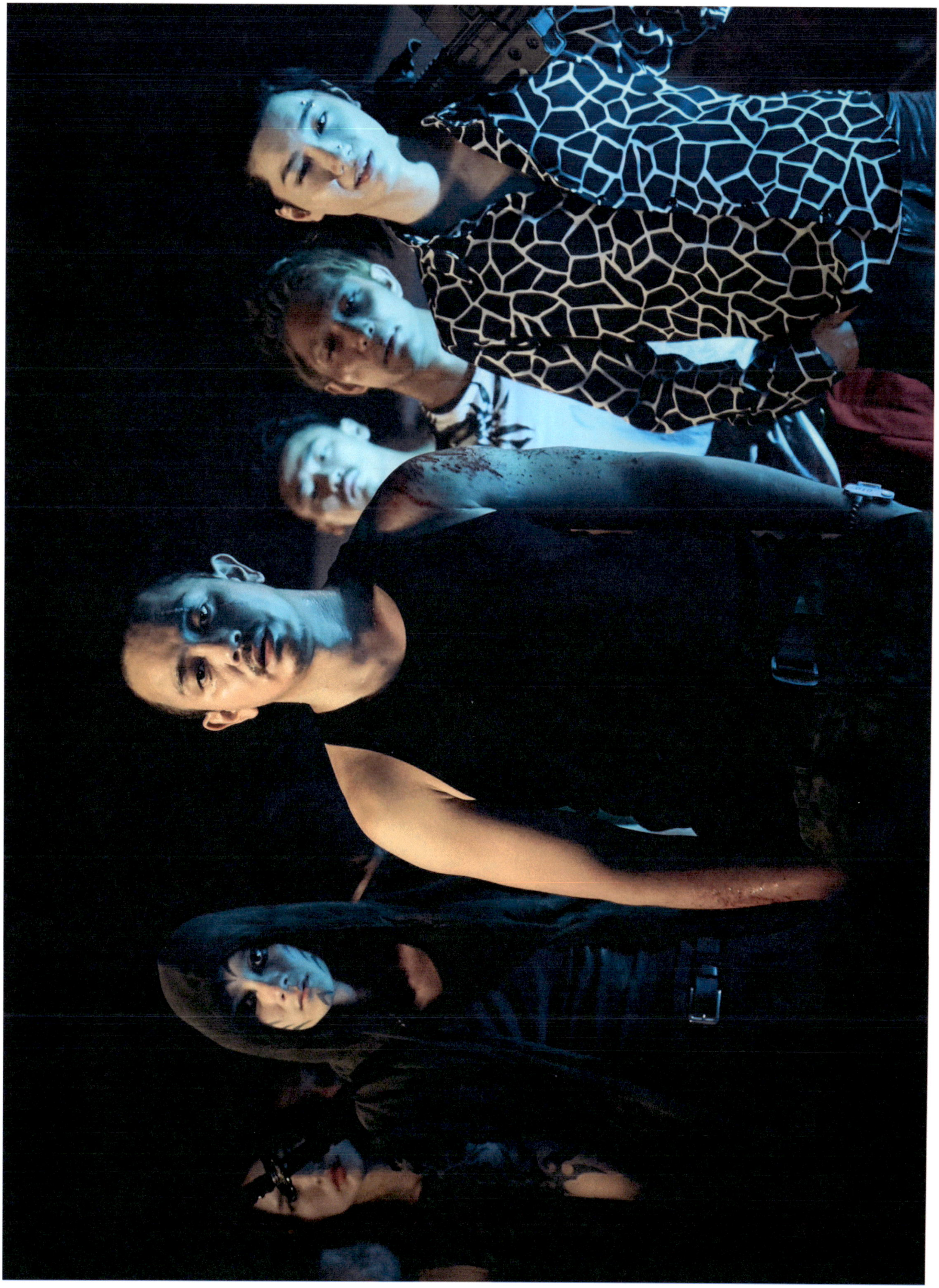

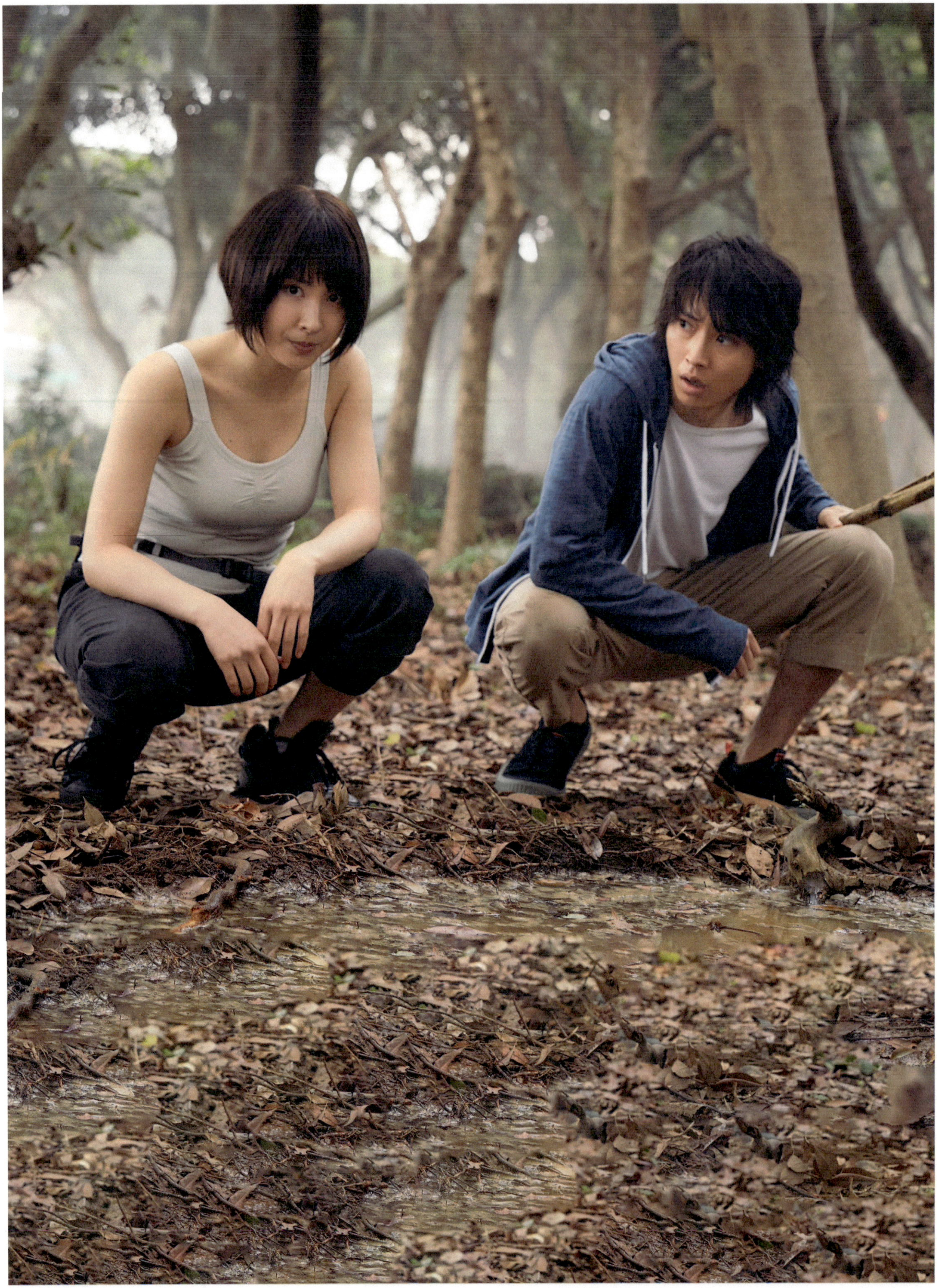

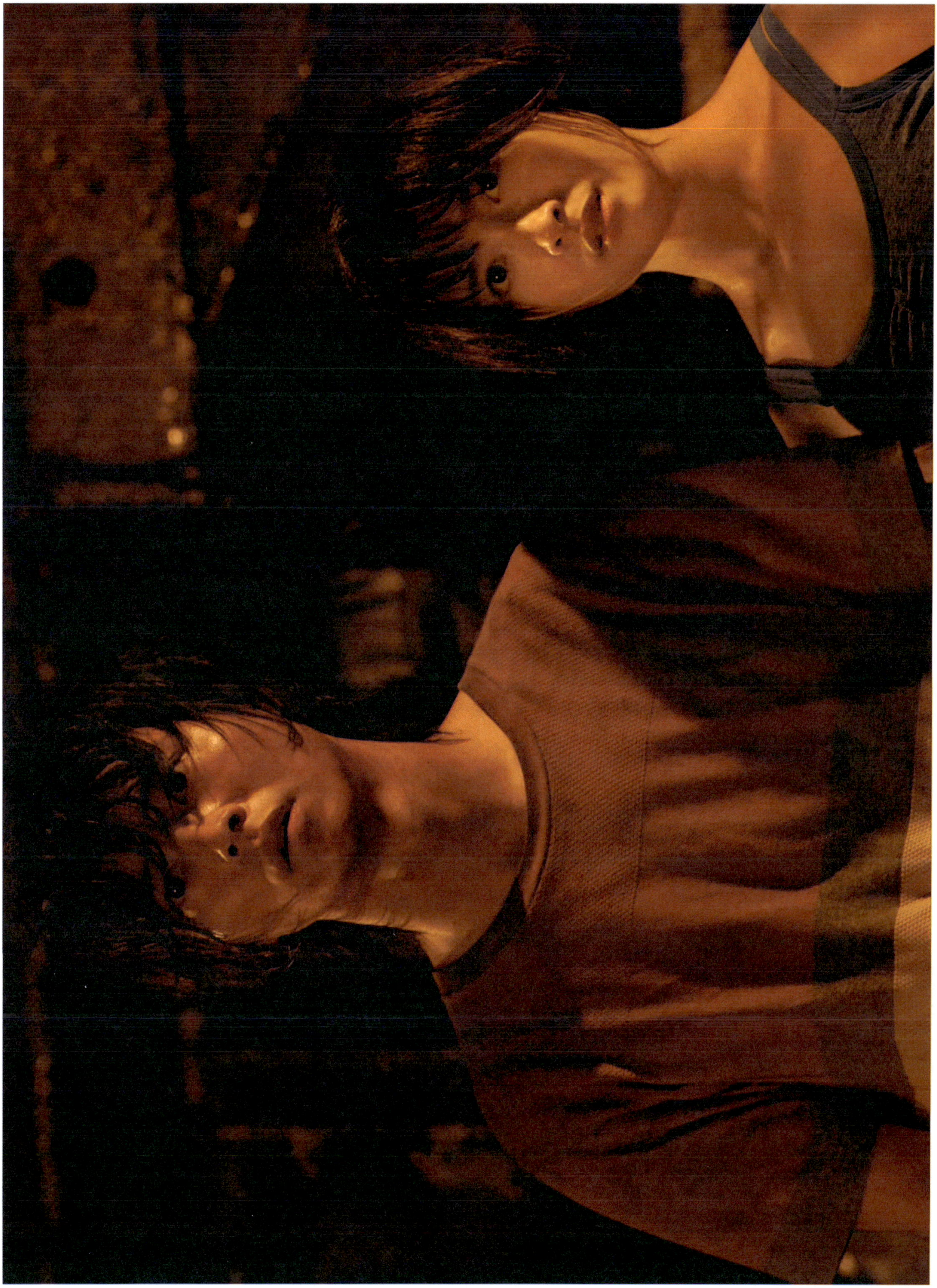

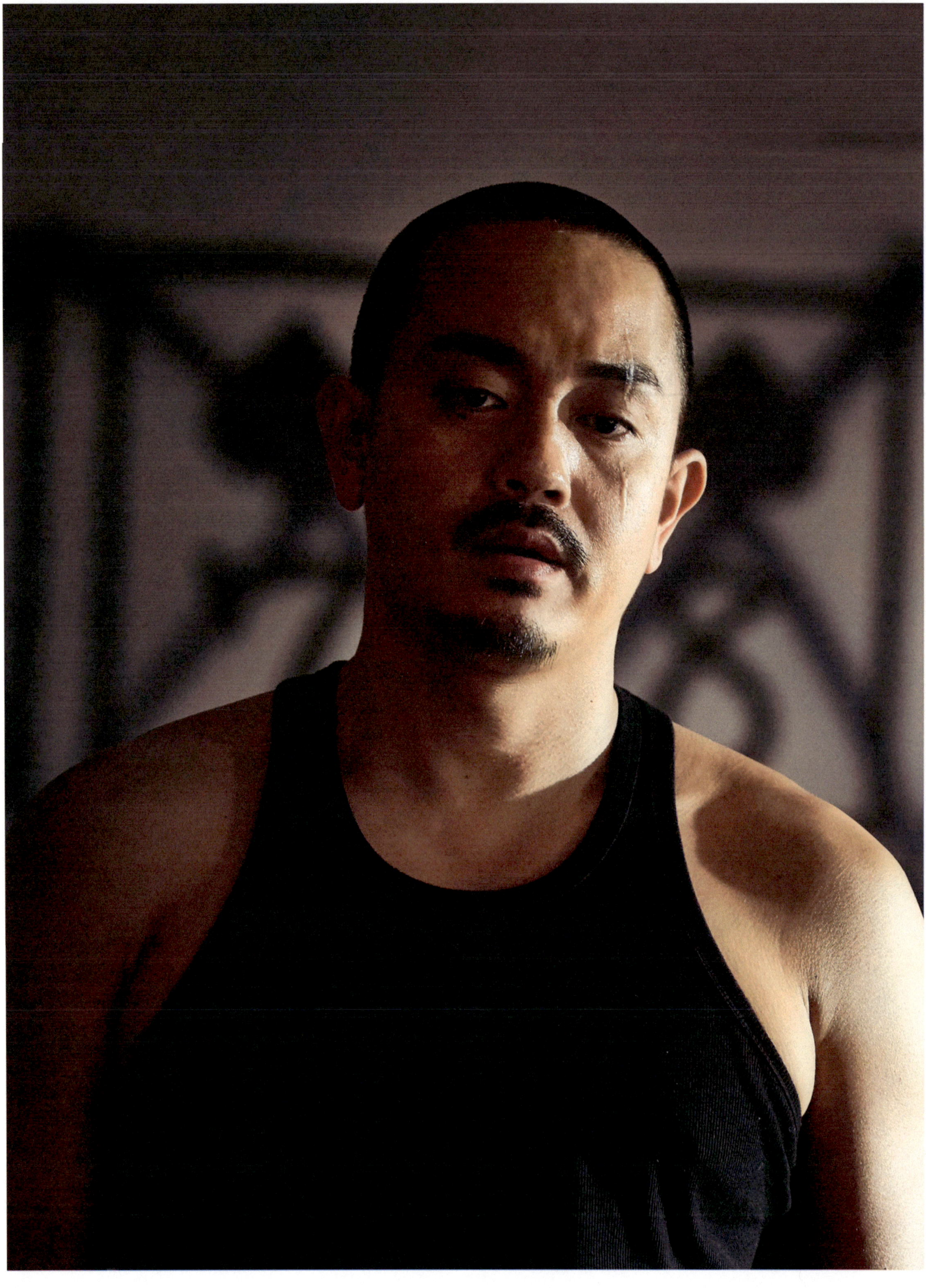

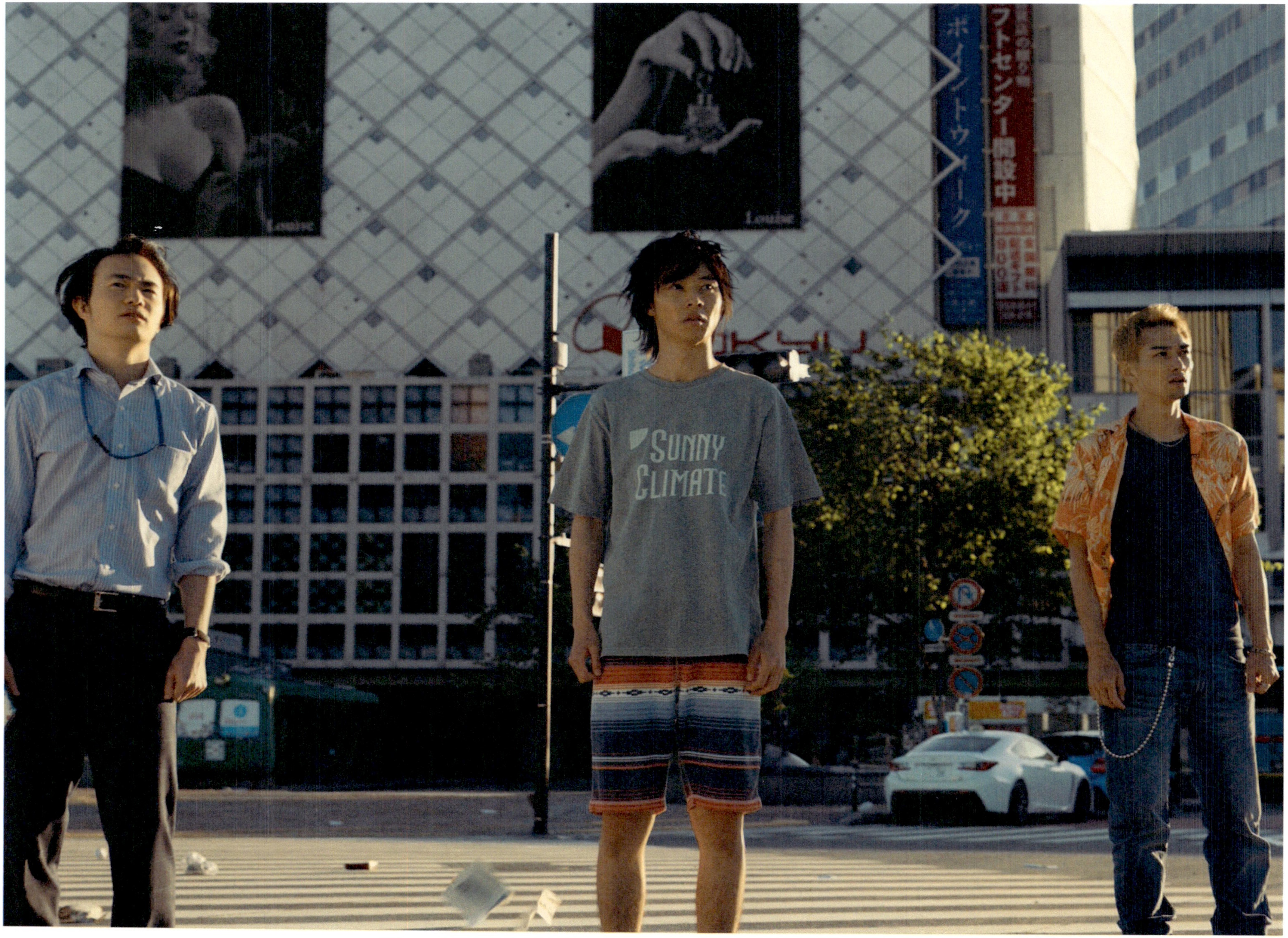
SUNNY CLIMATE
ポイントウィーク
フトセンター開設中
Louise
Louise

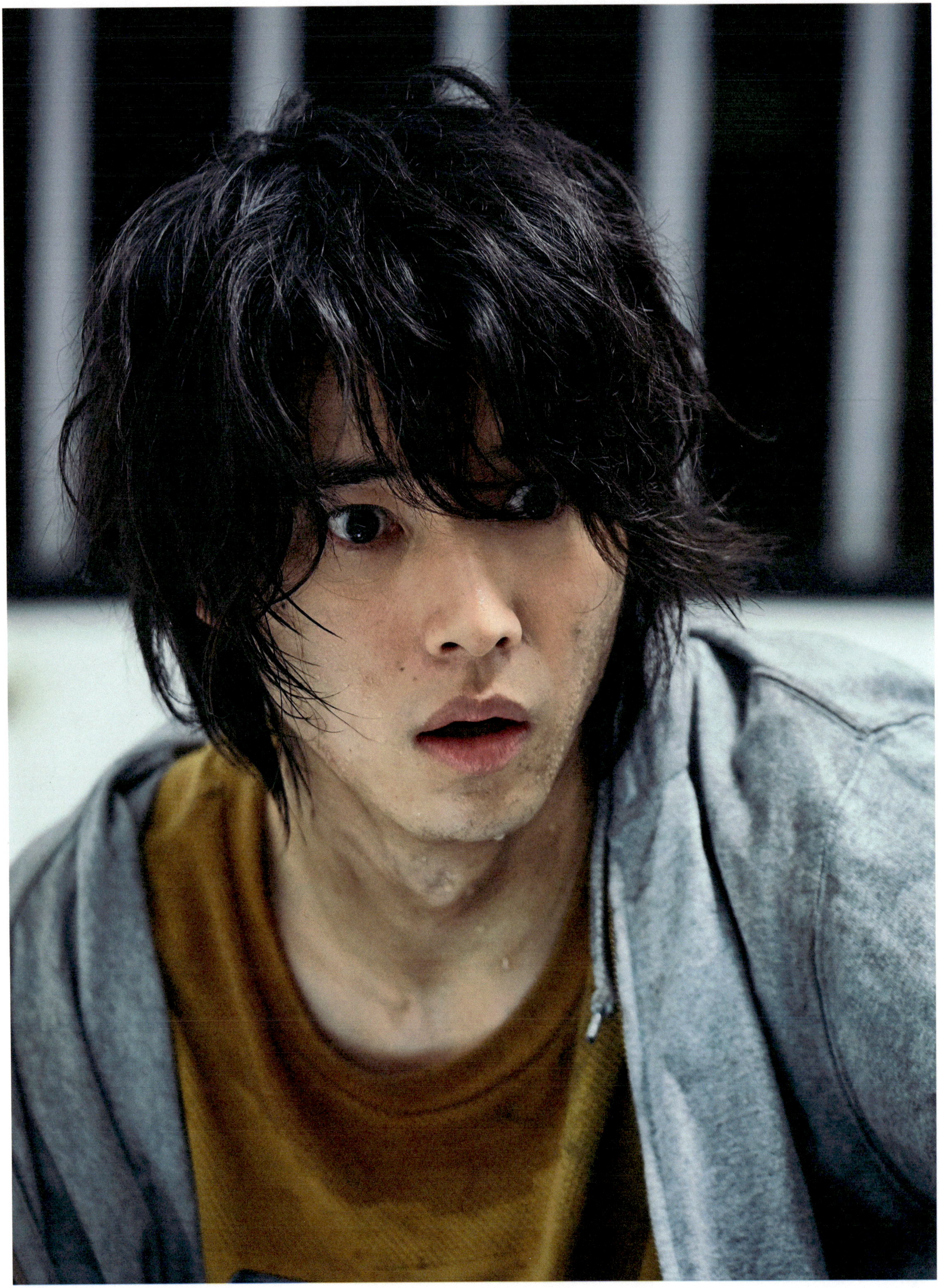

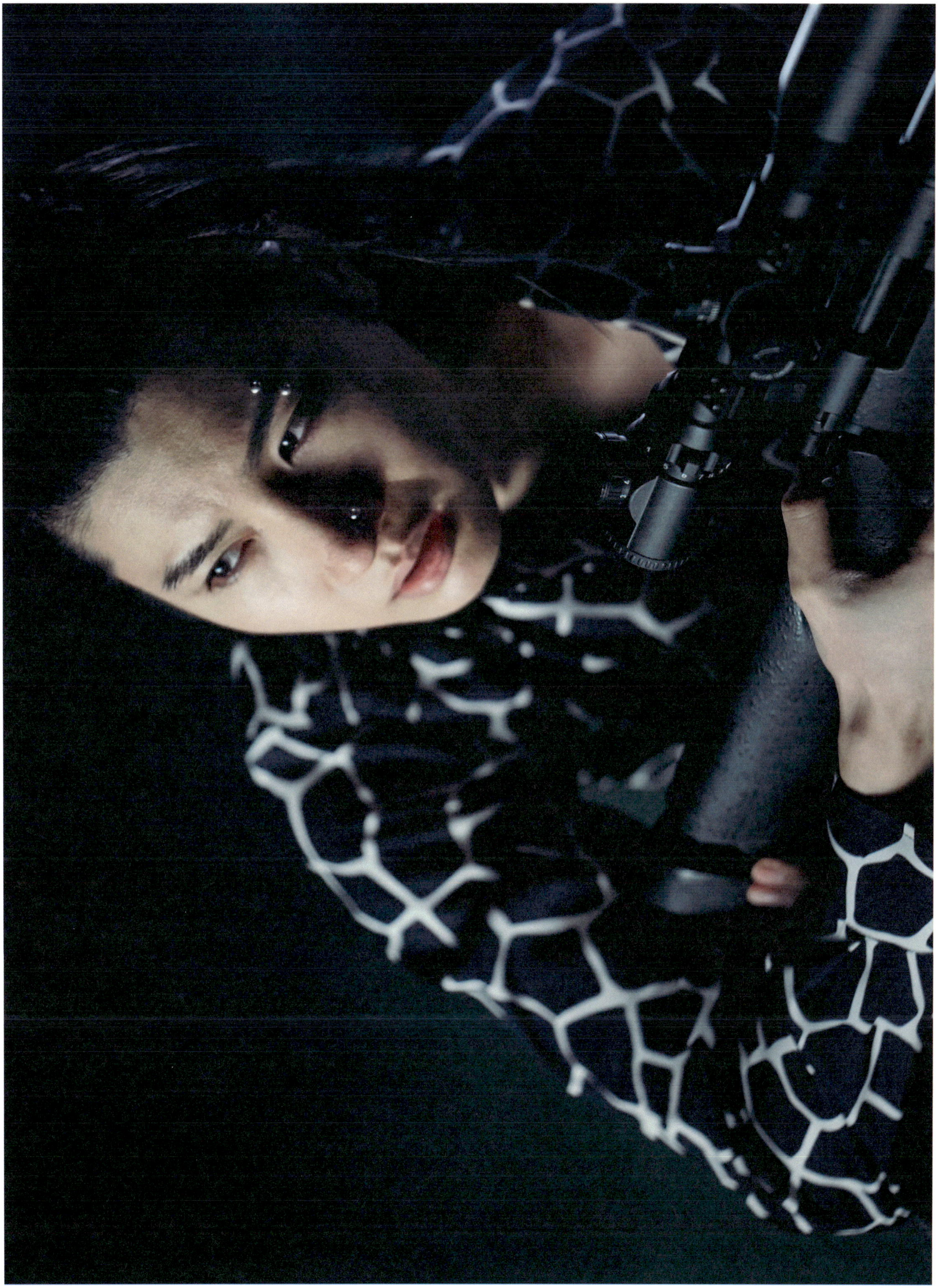

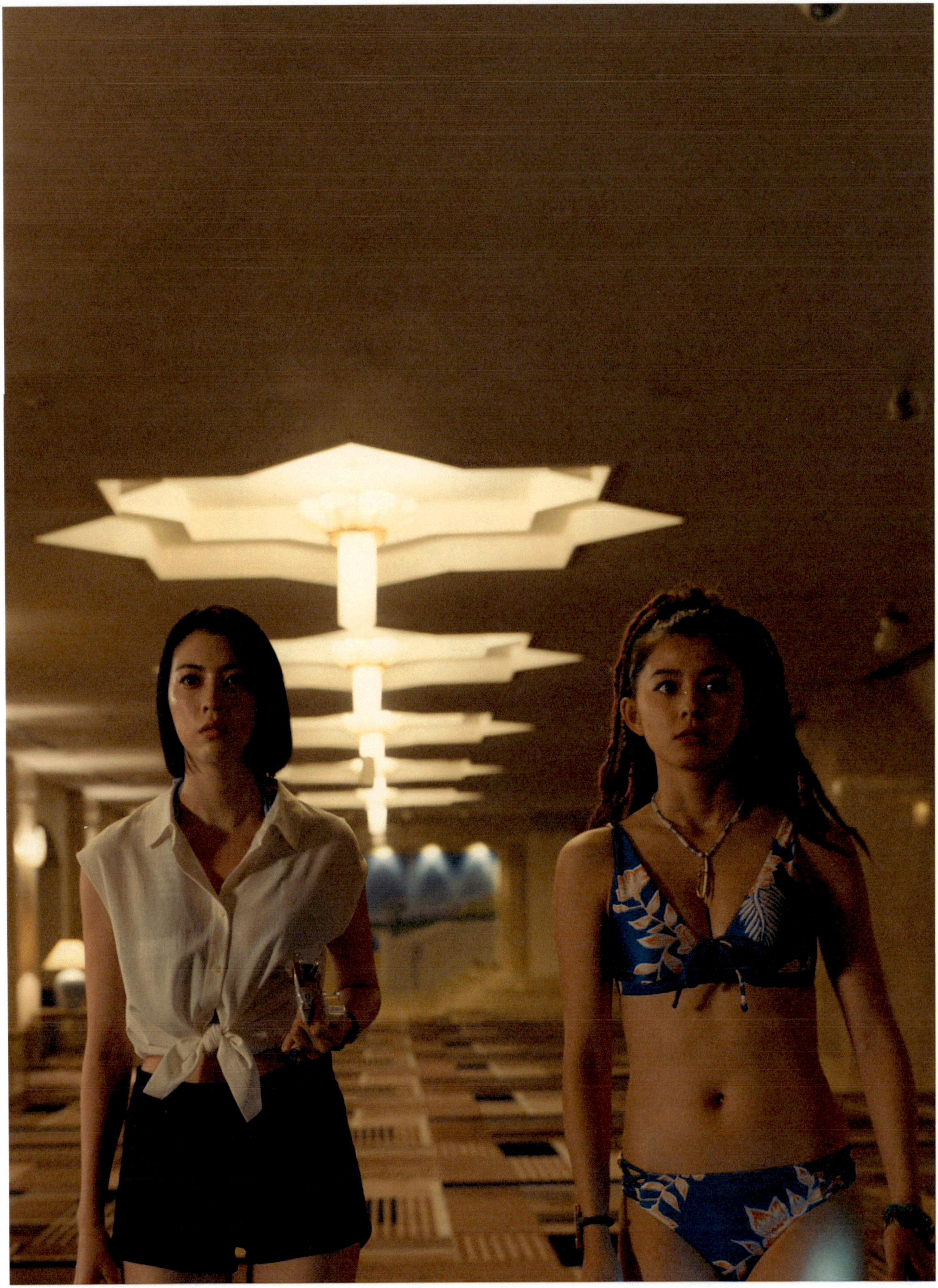

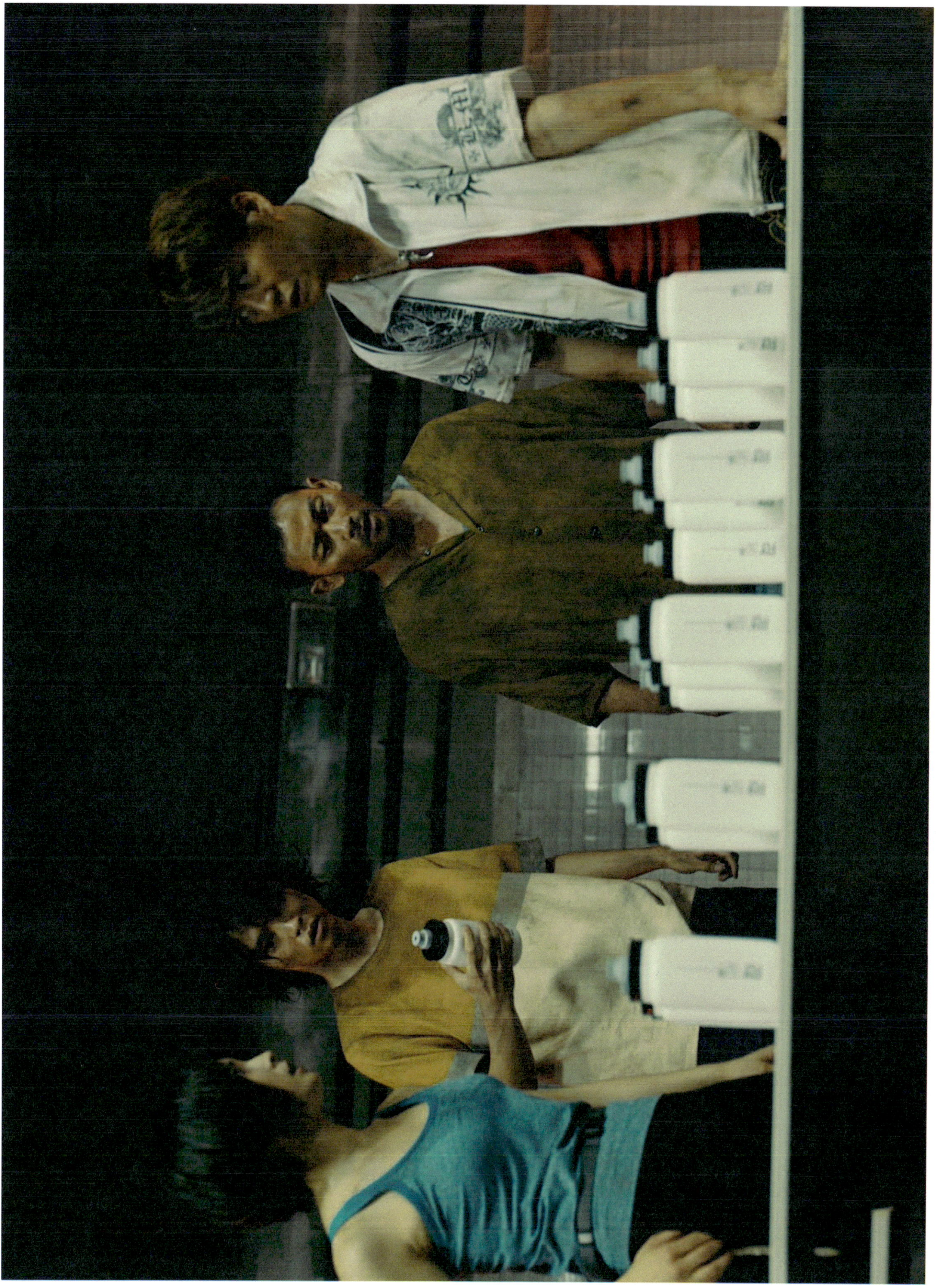

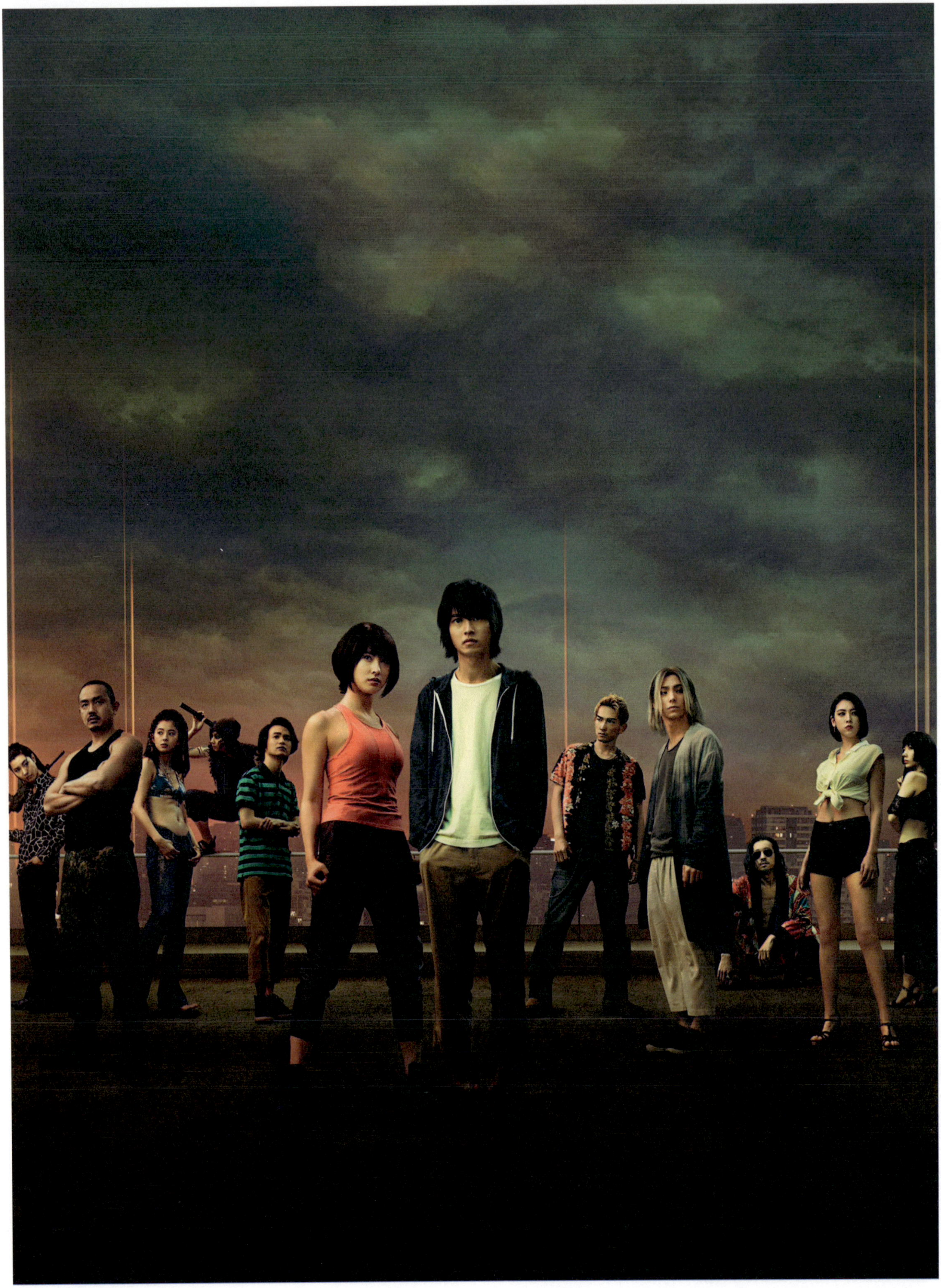

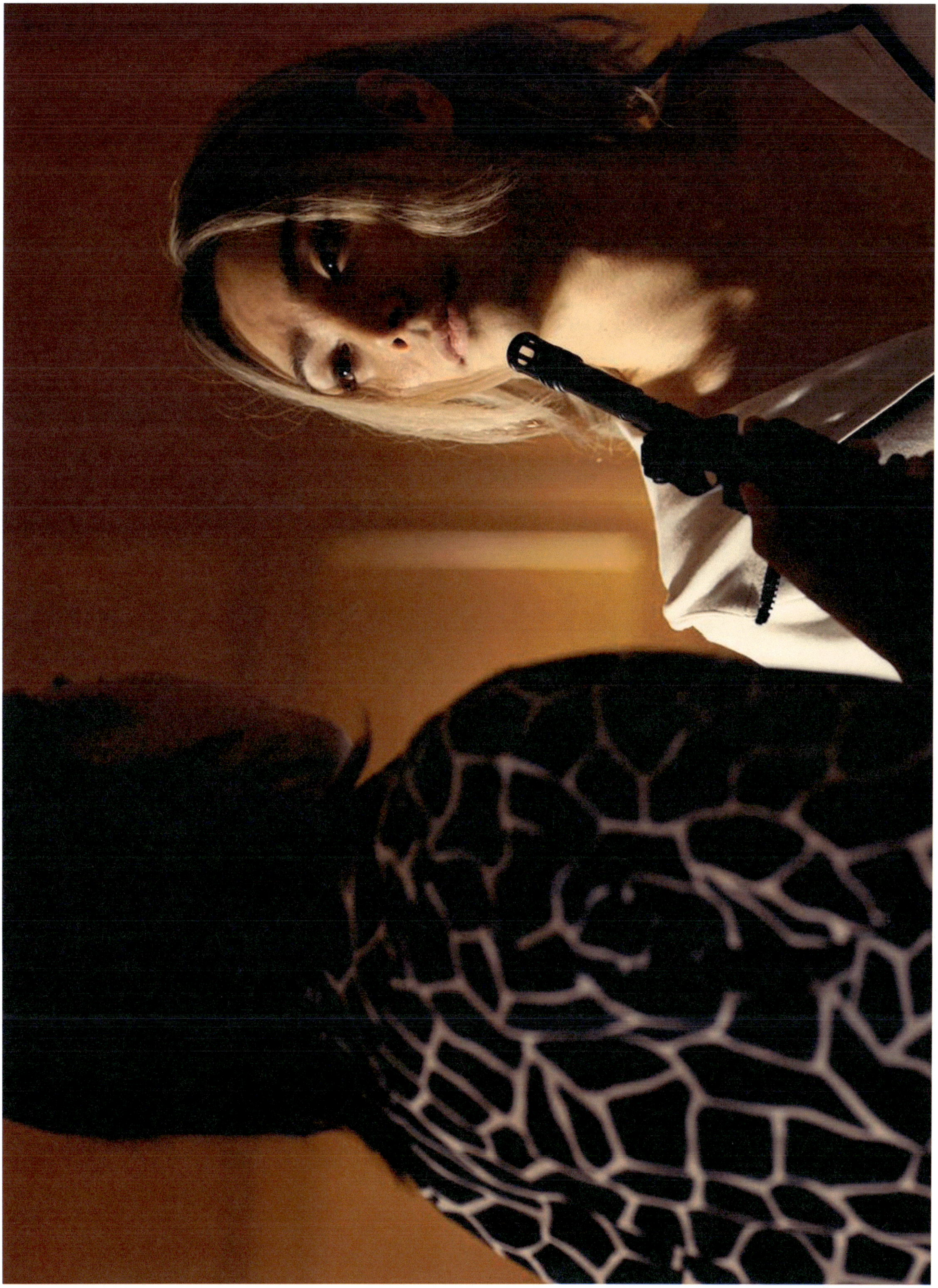

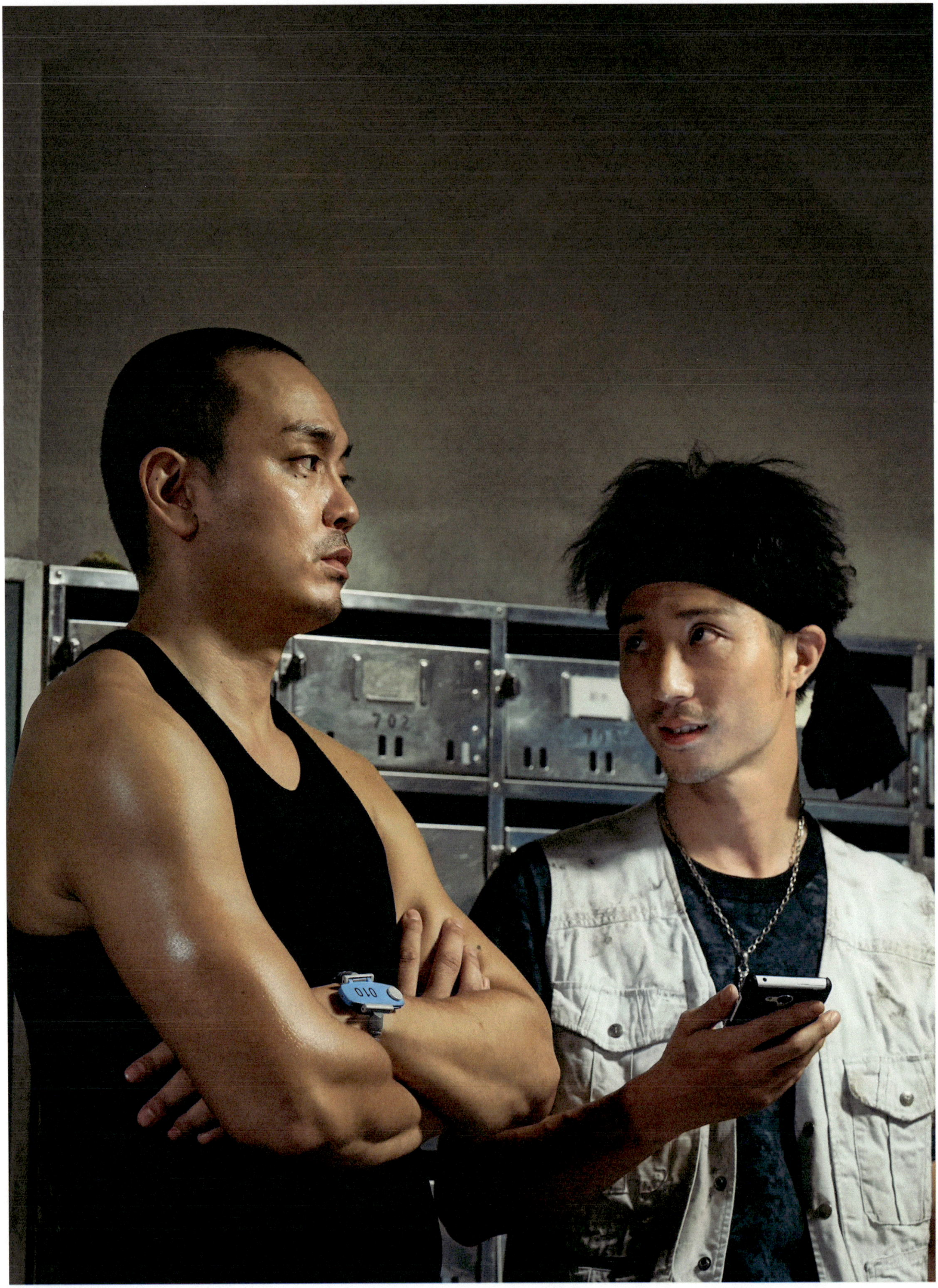
702

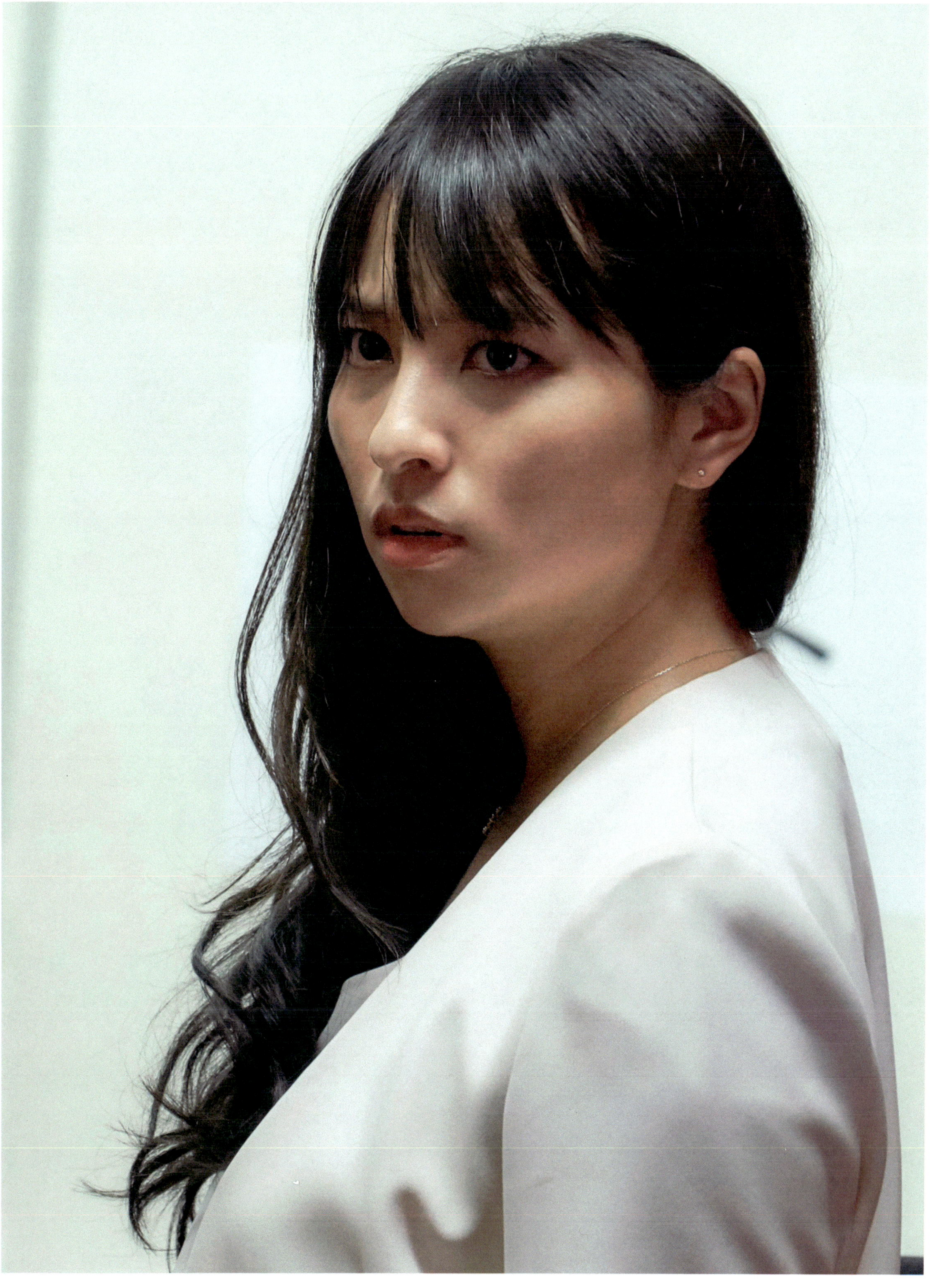

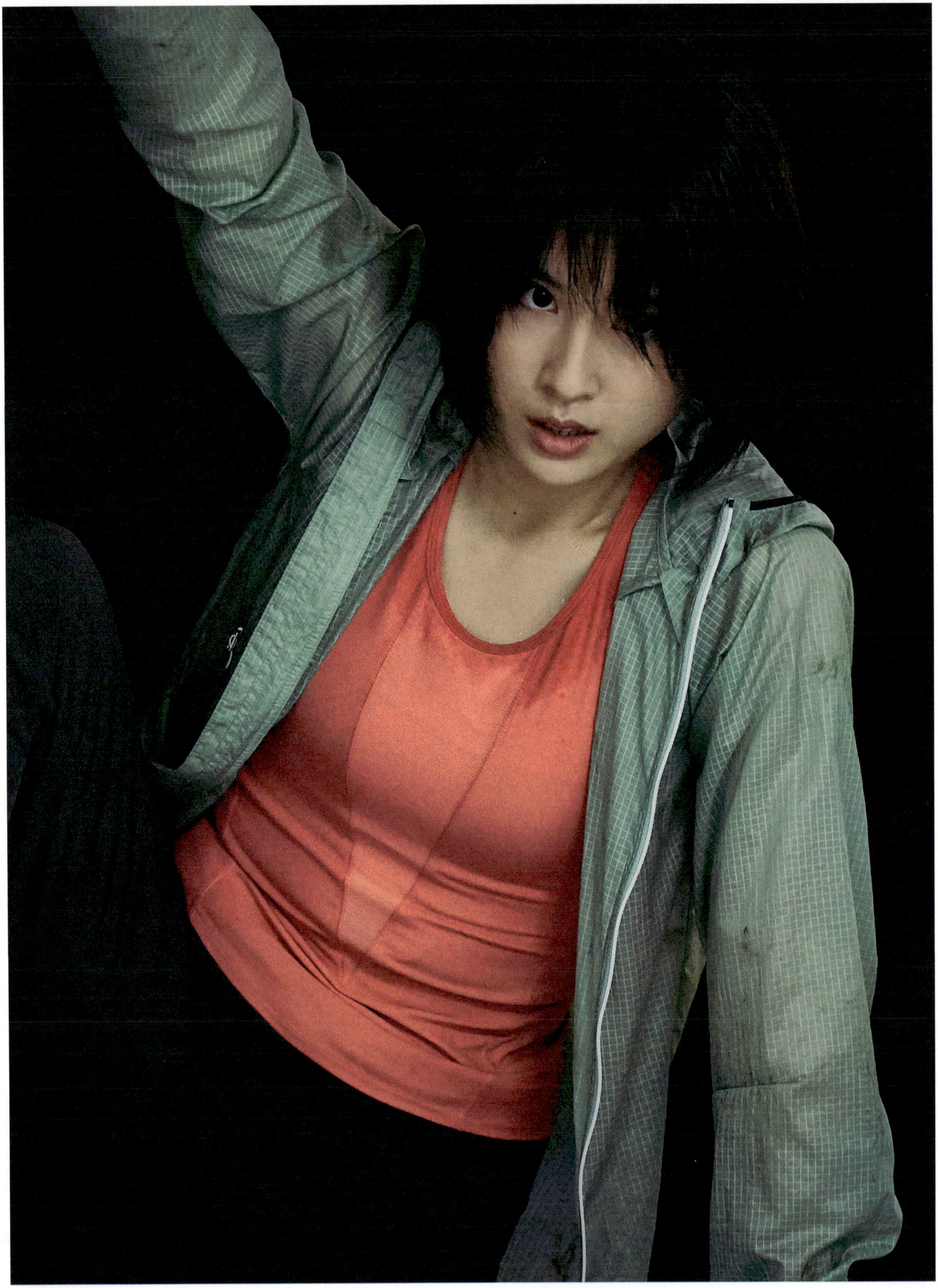

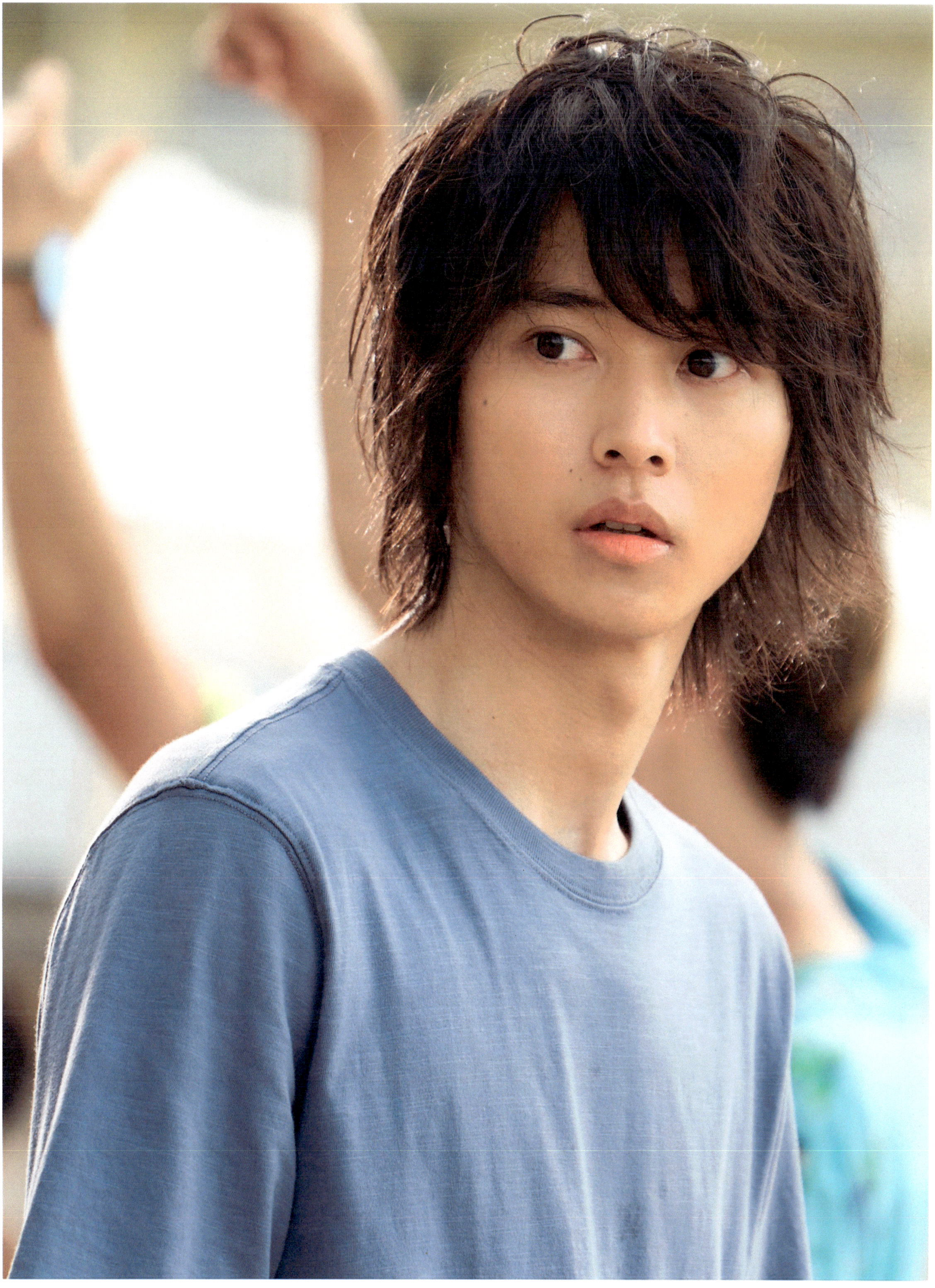

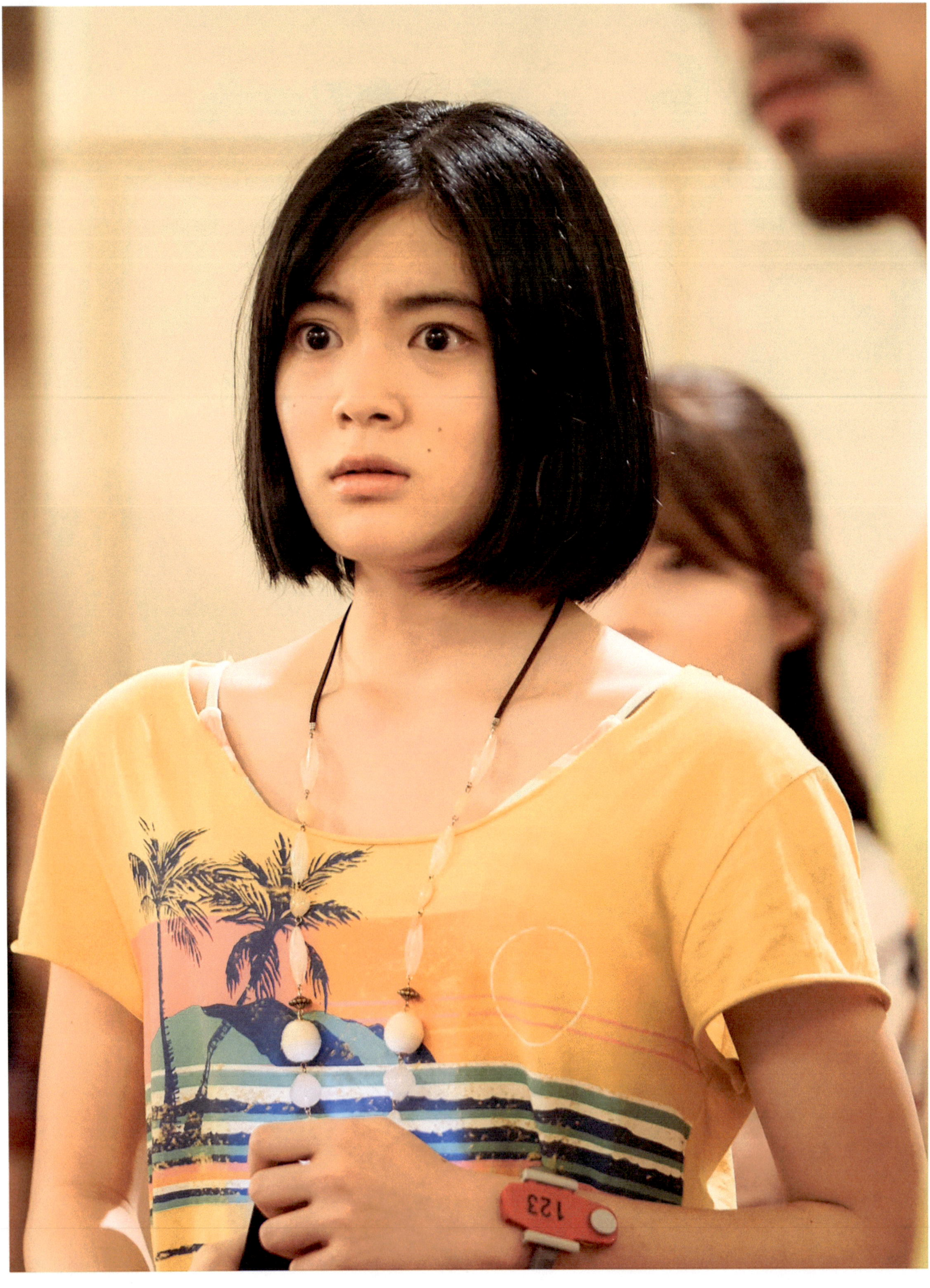
123

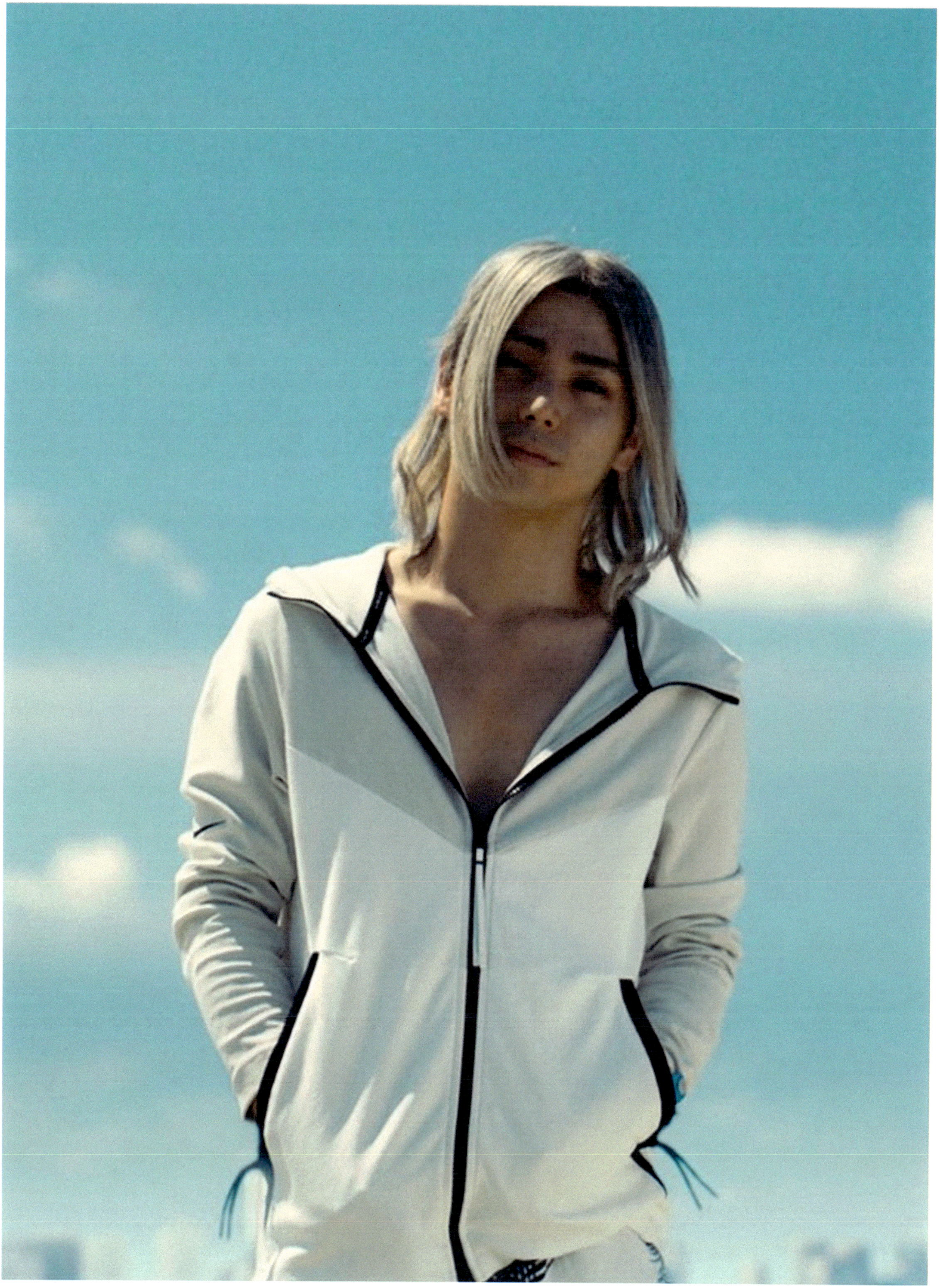

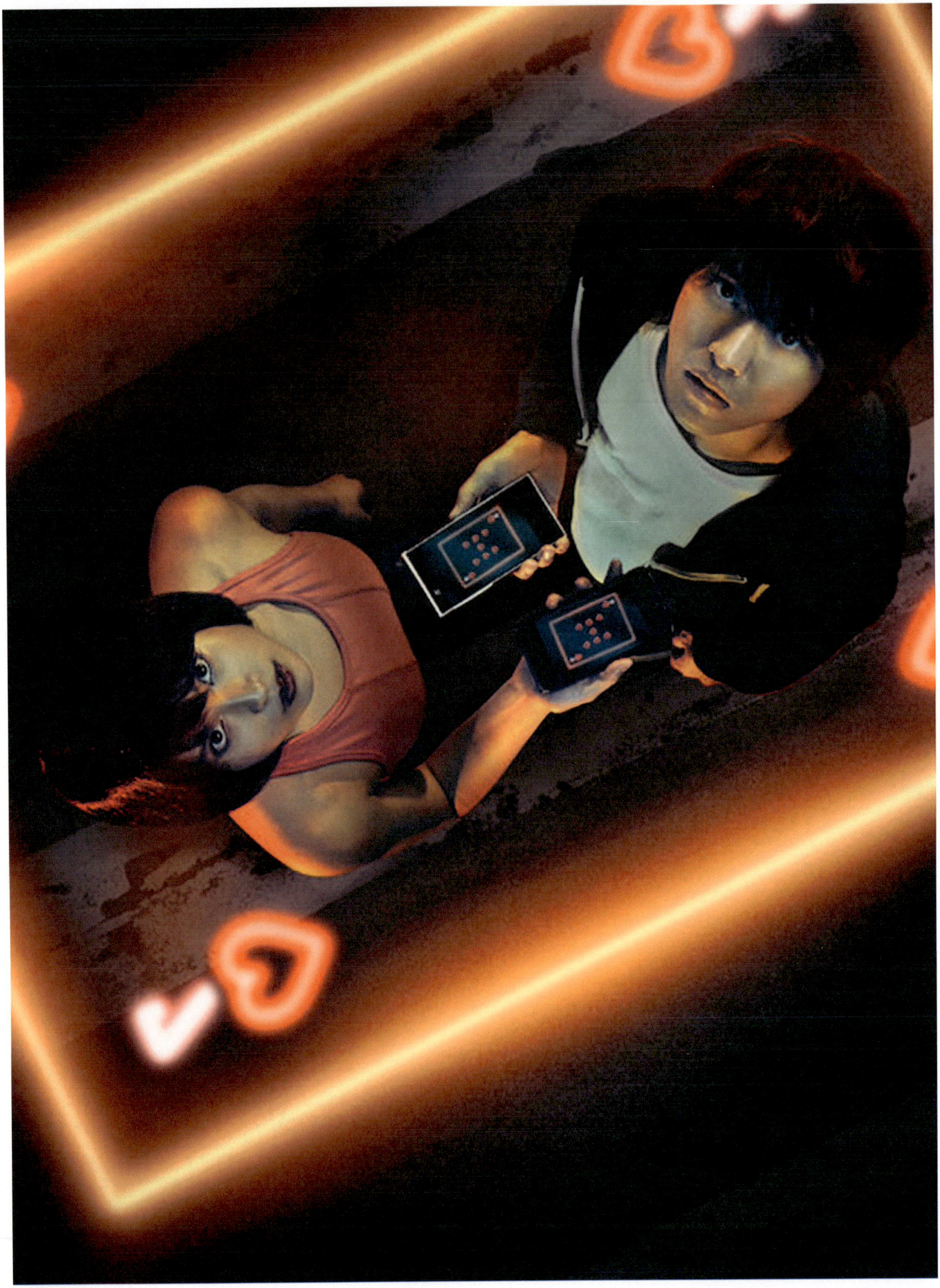

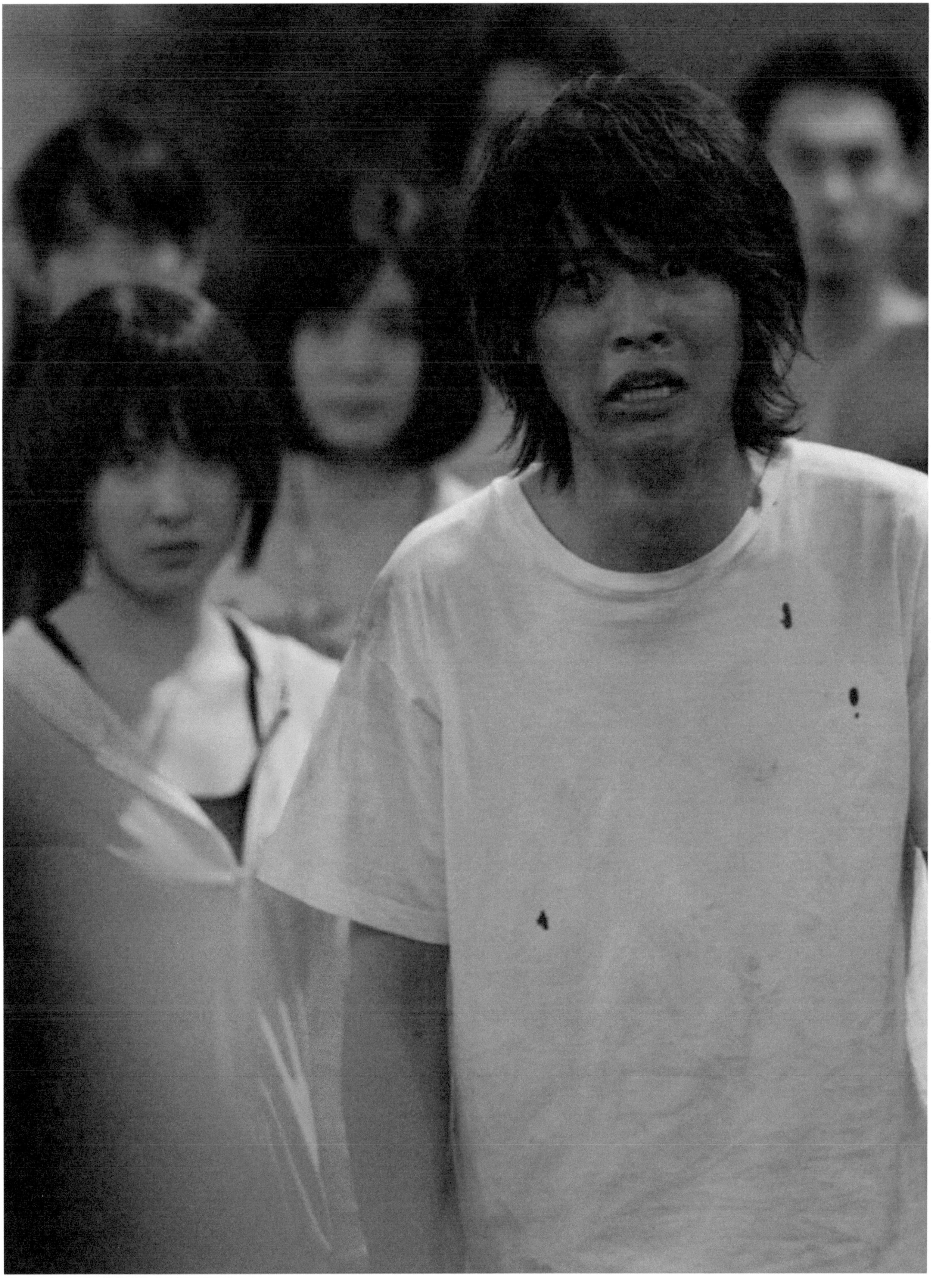

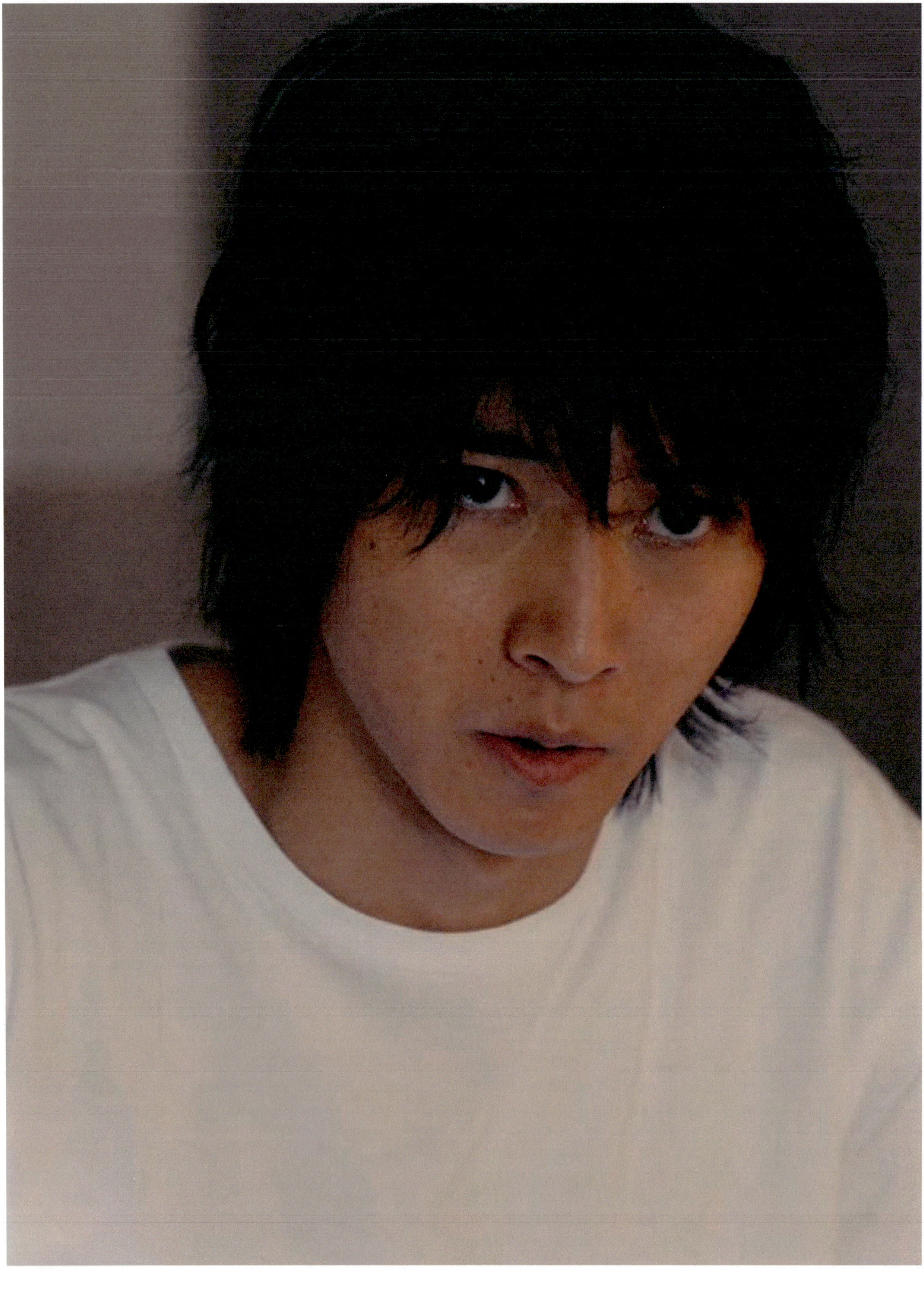

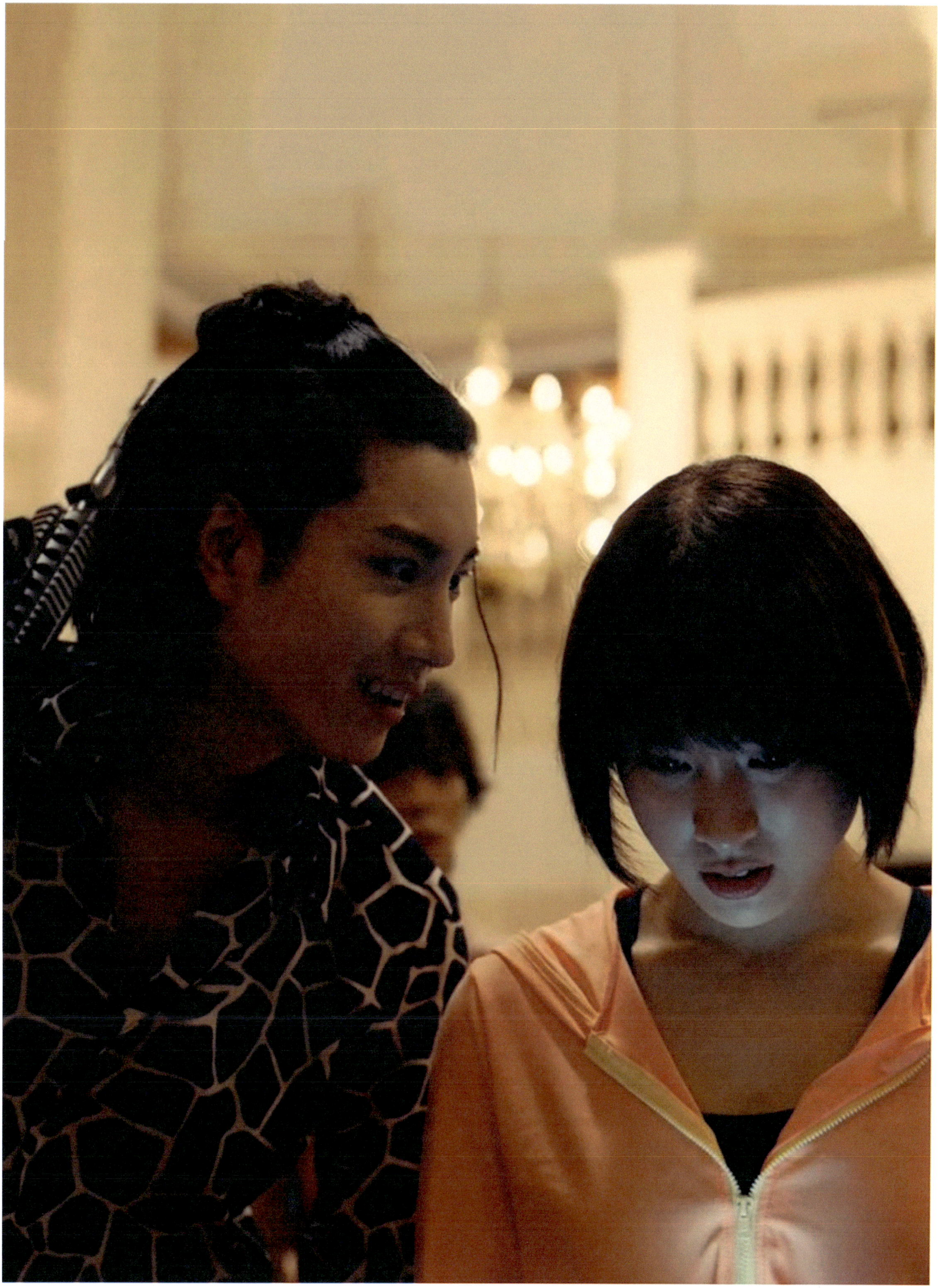

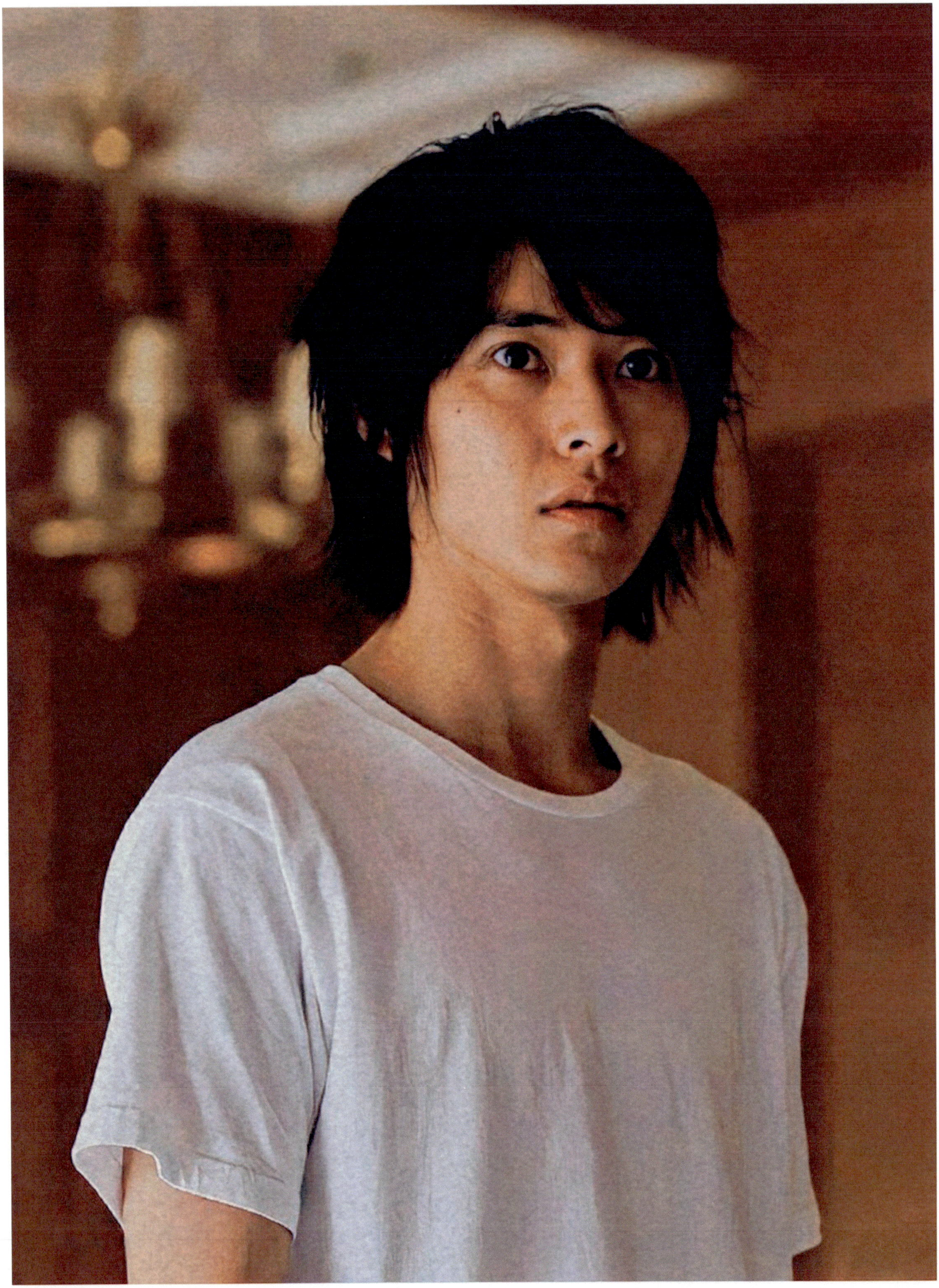

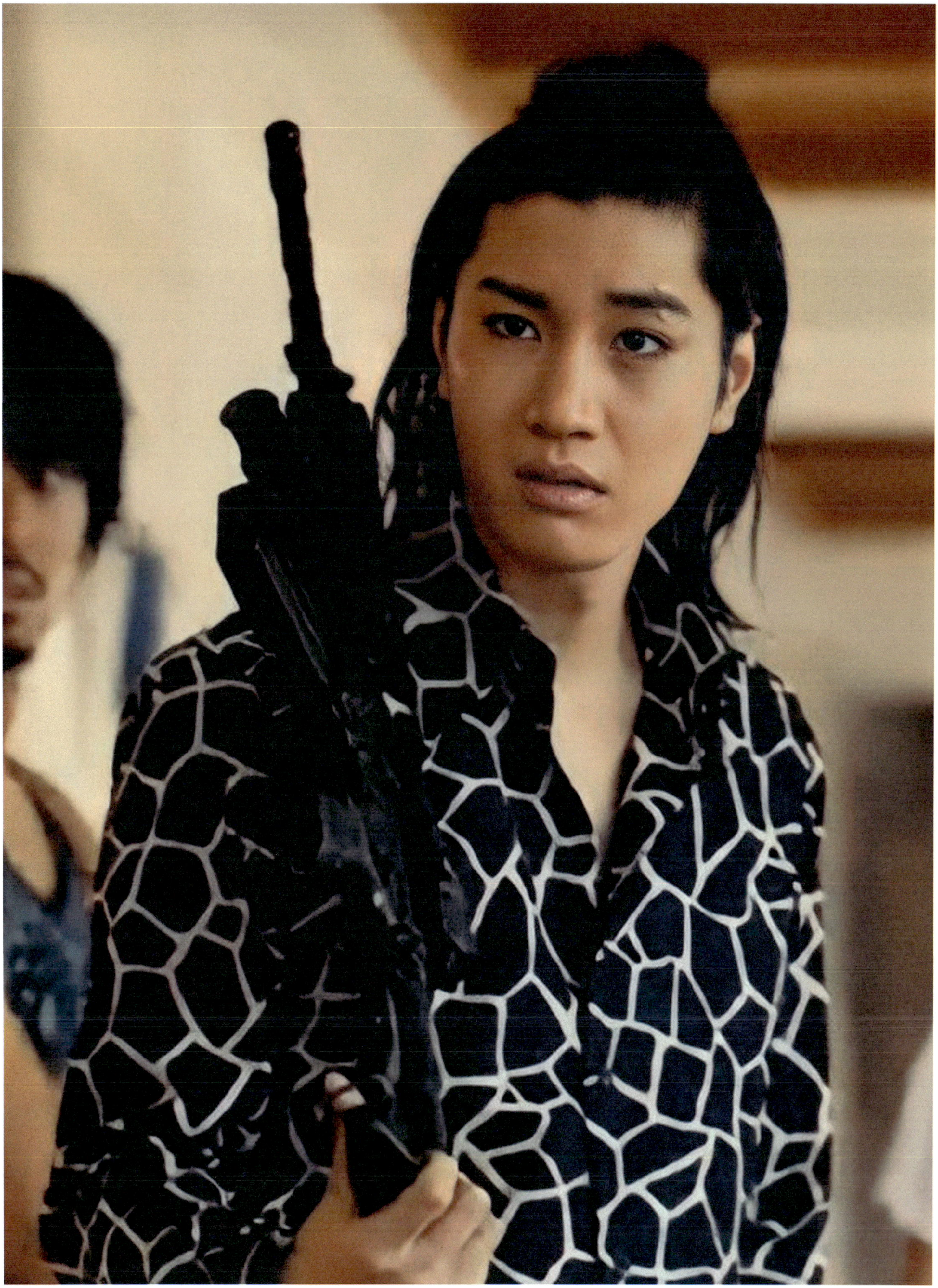

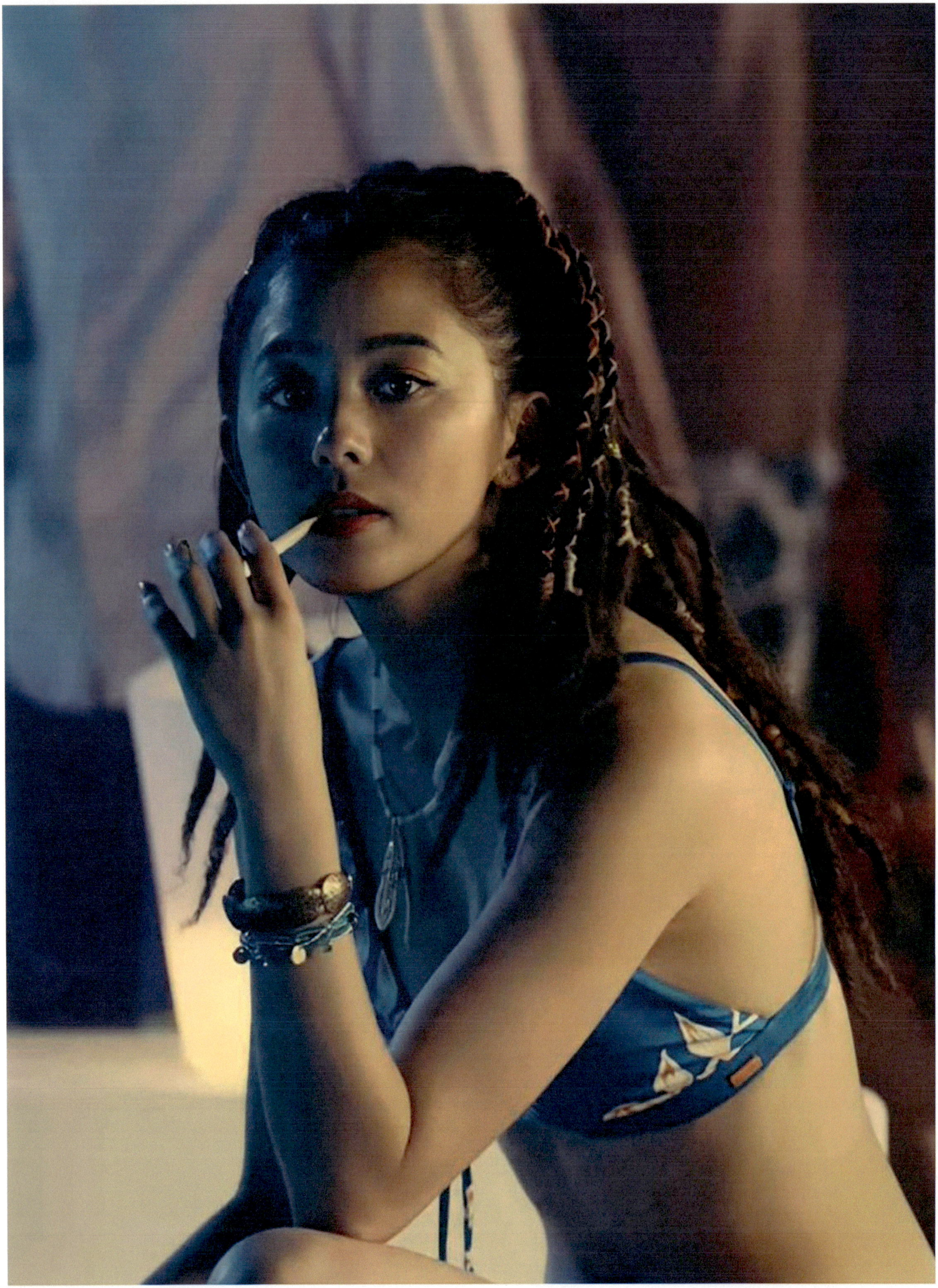

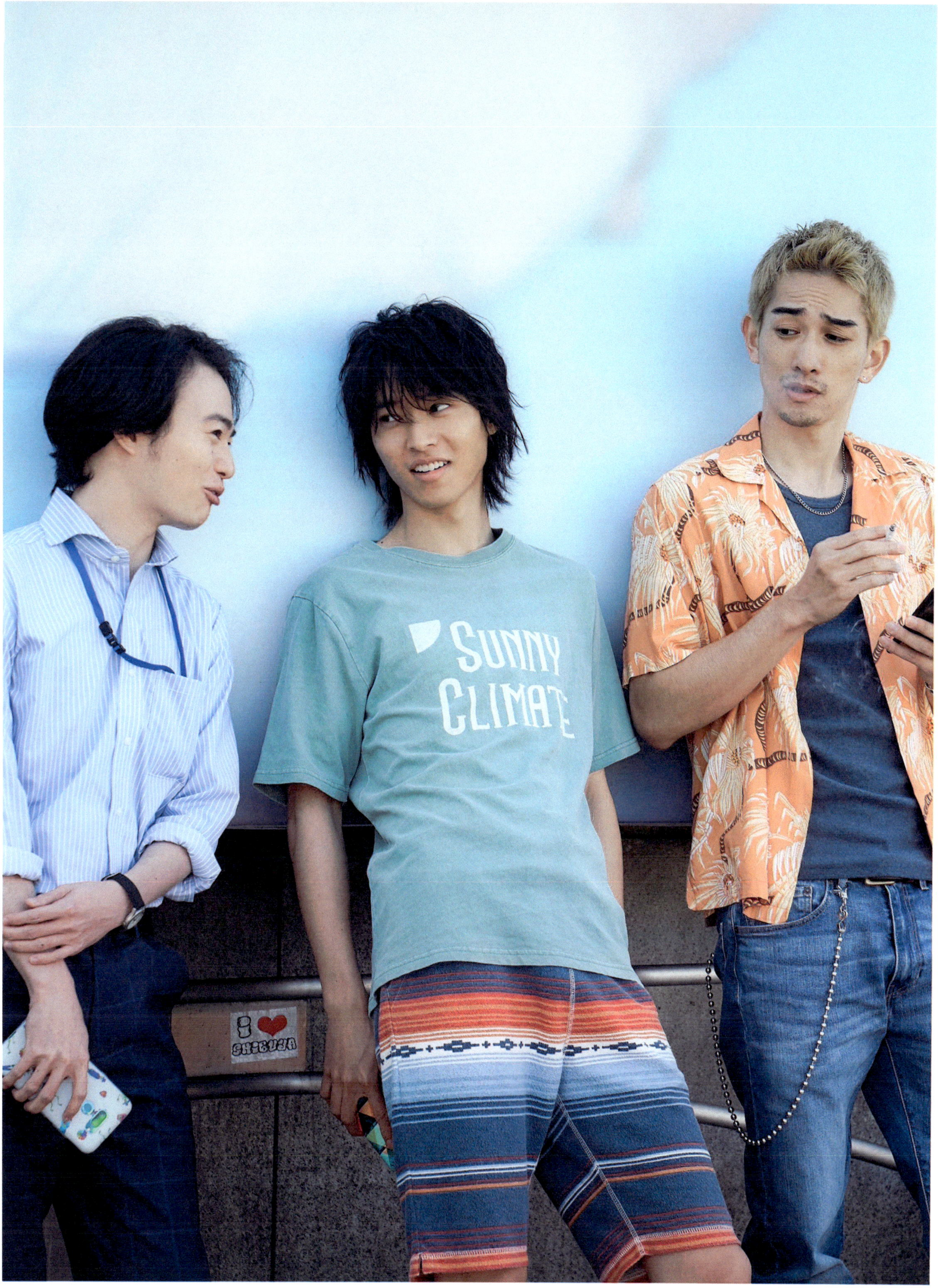
SUNNY
CLIMATE

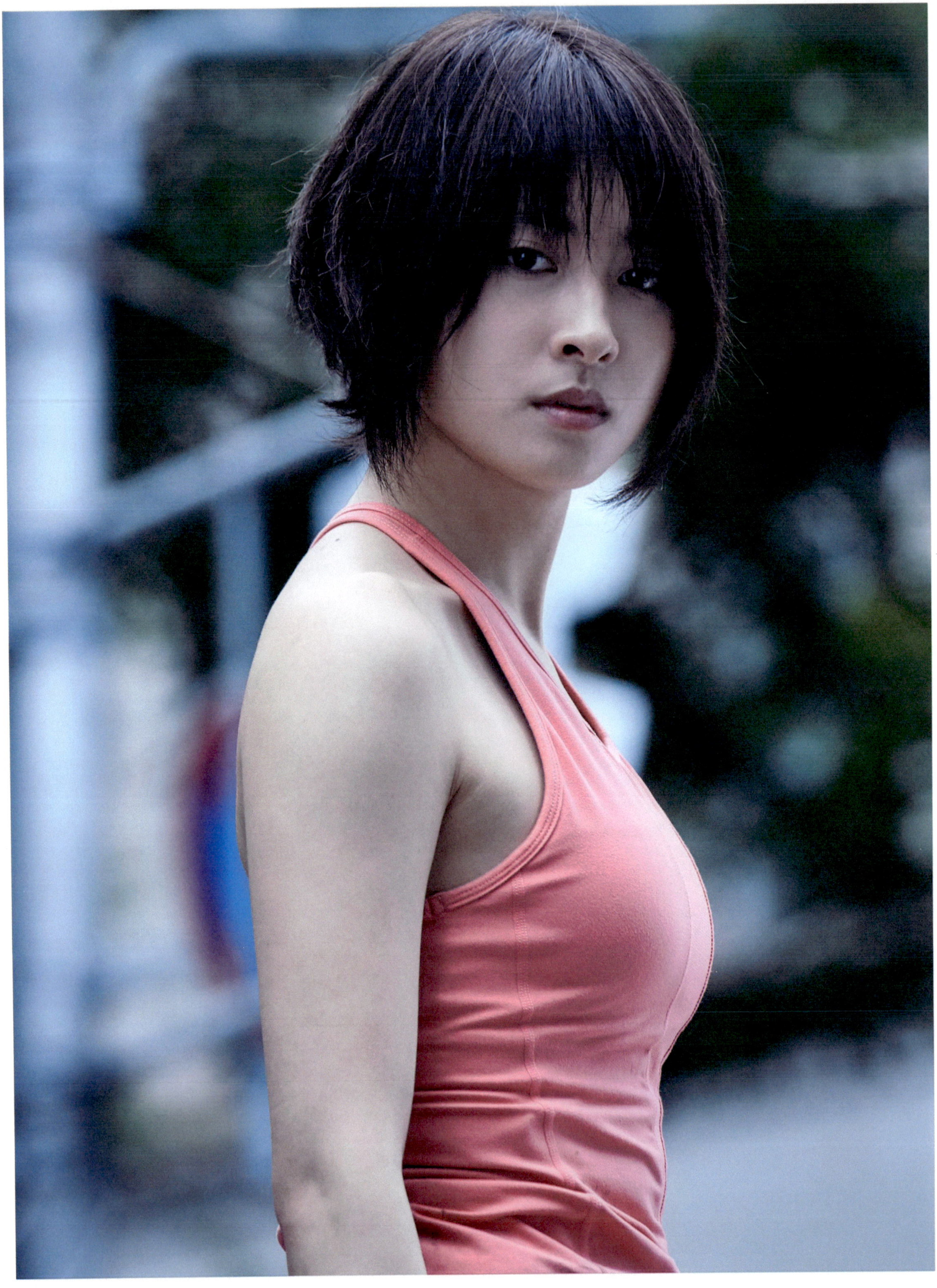

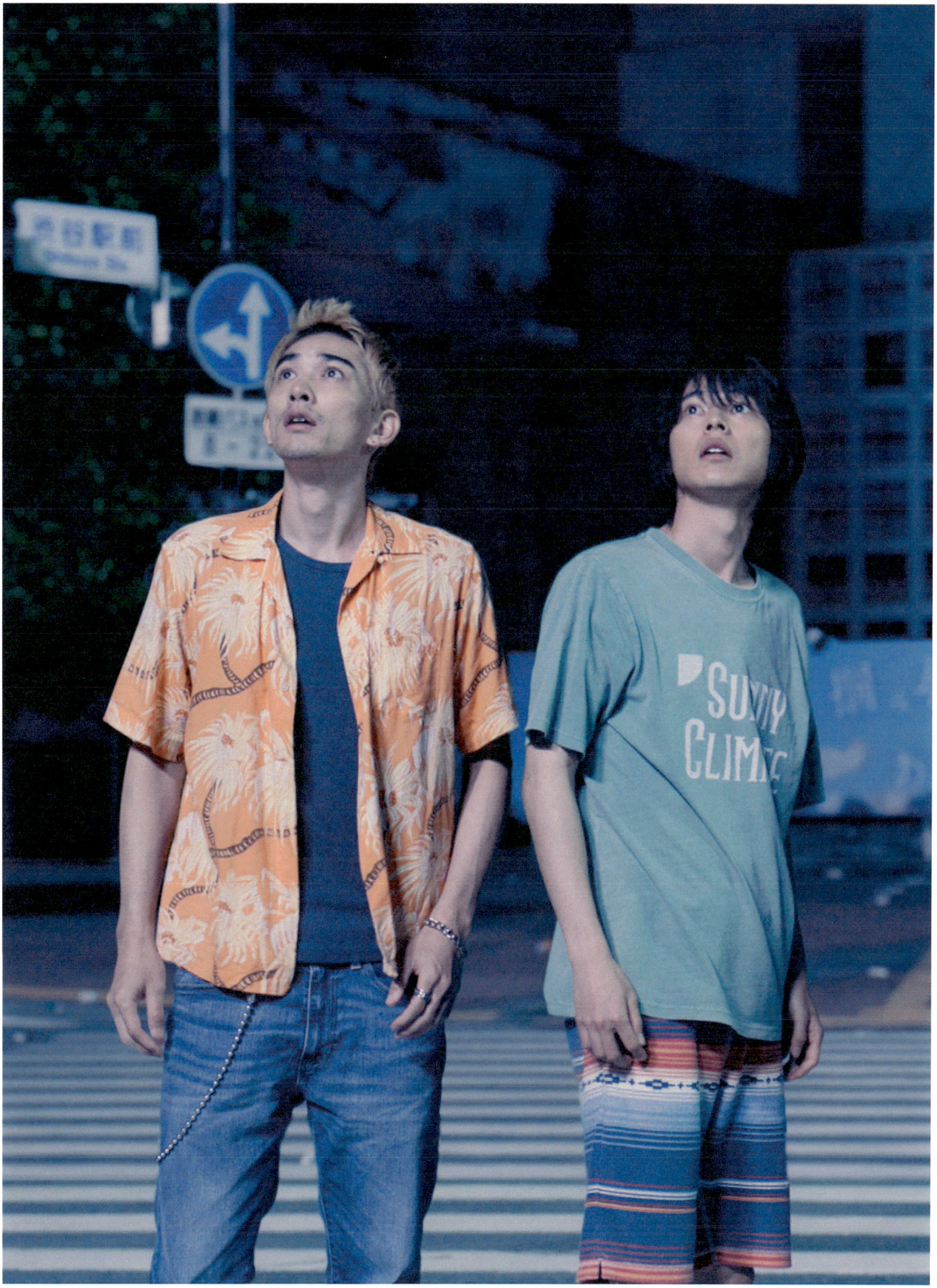

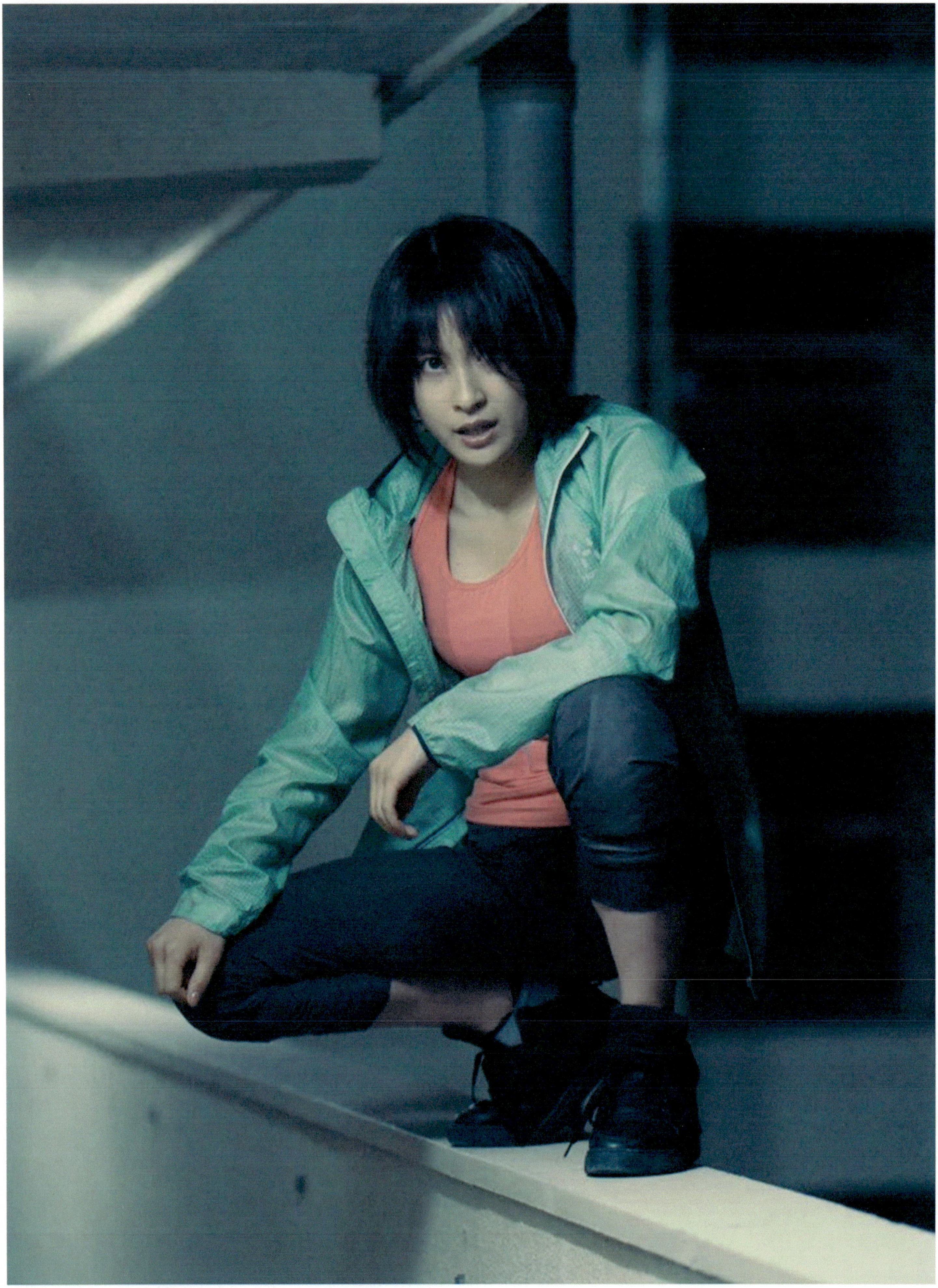

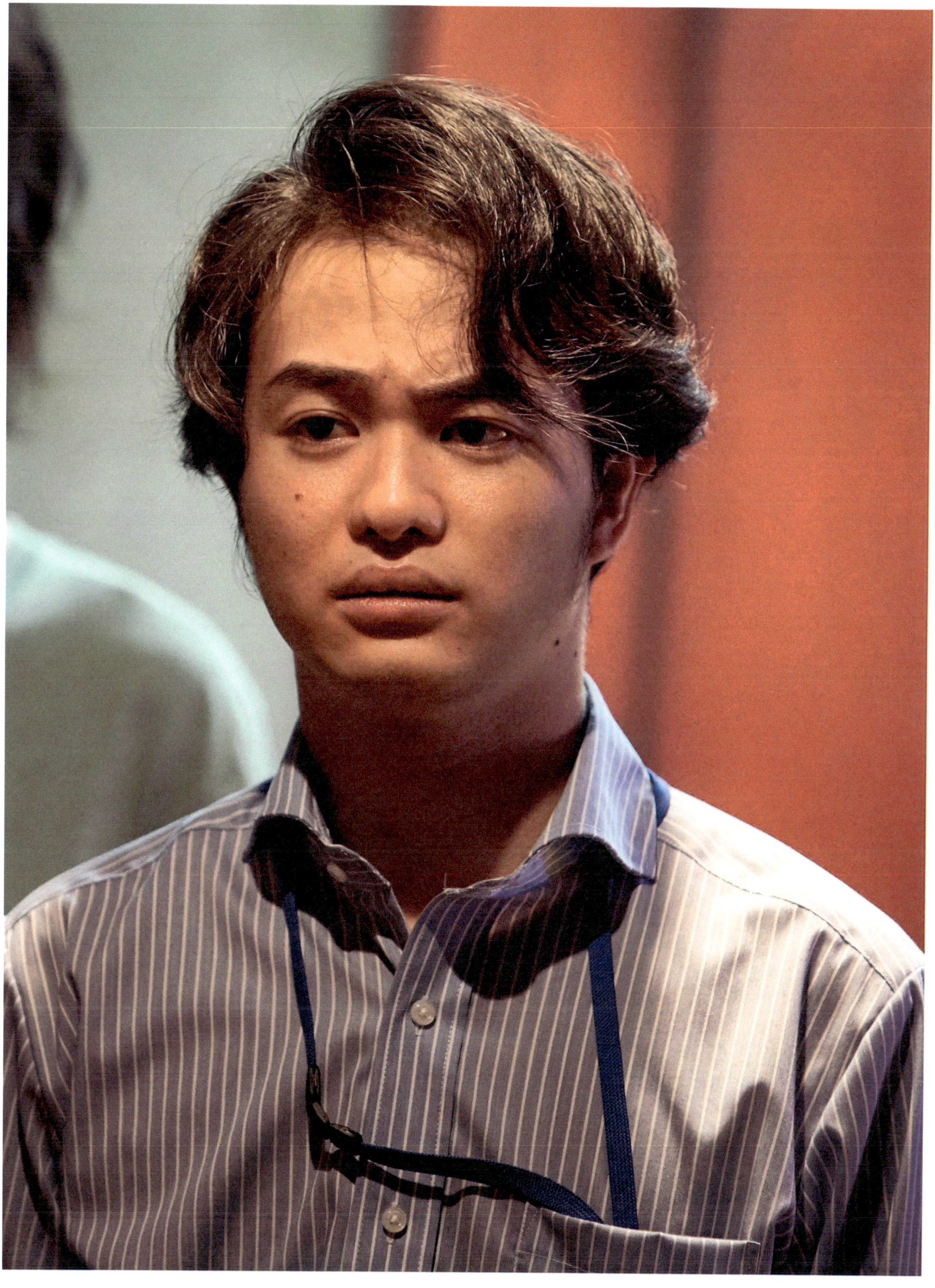

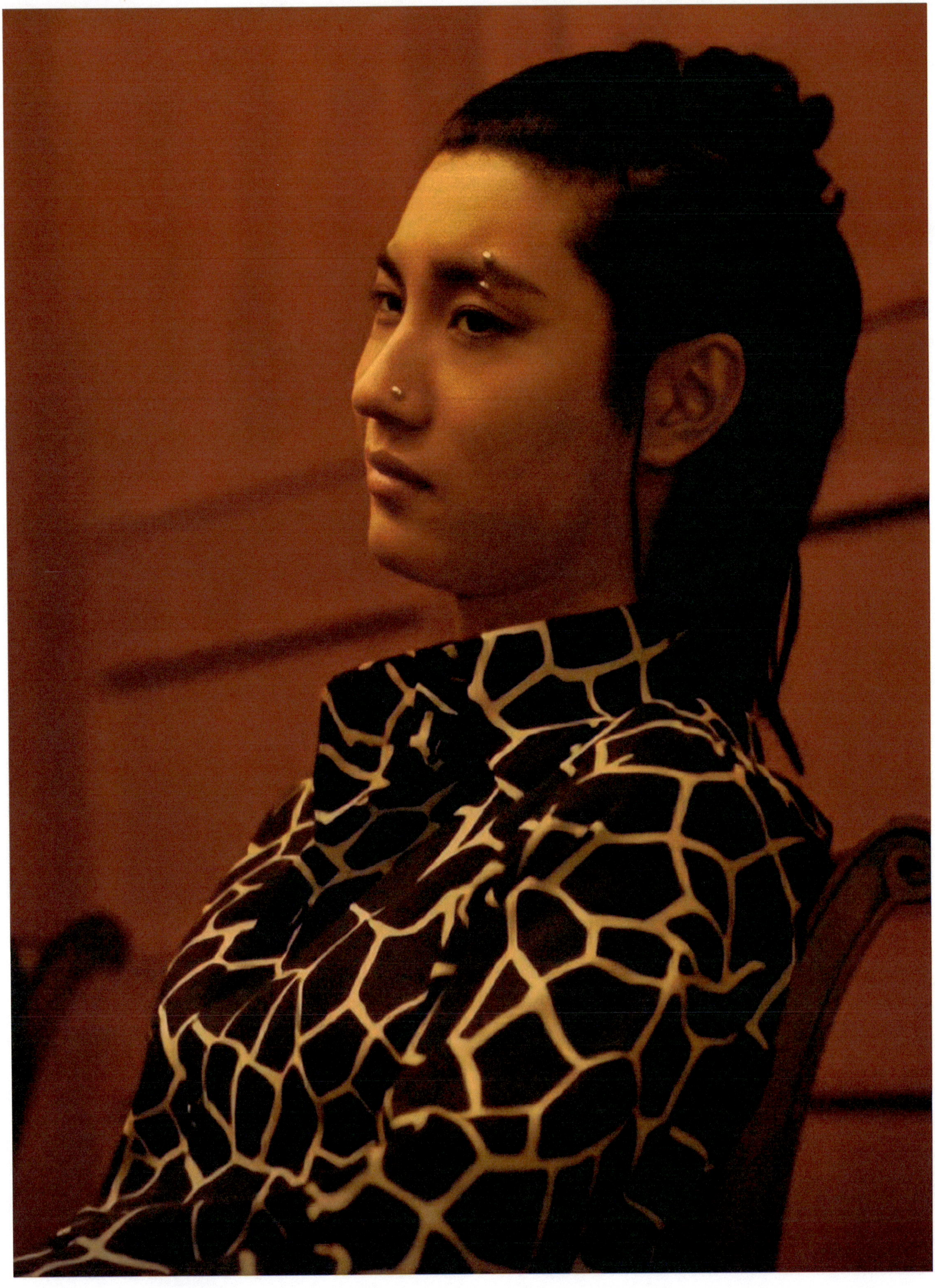

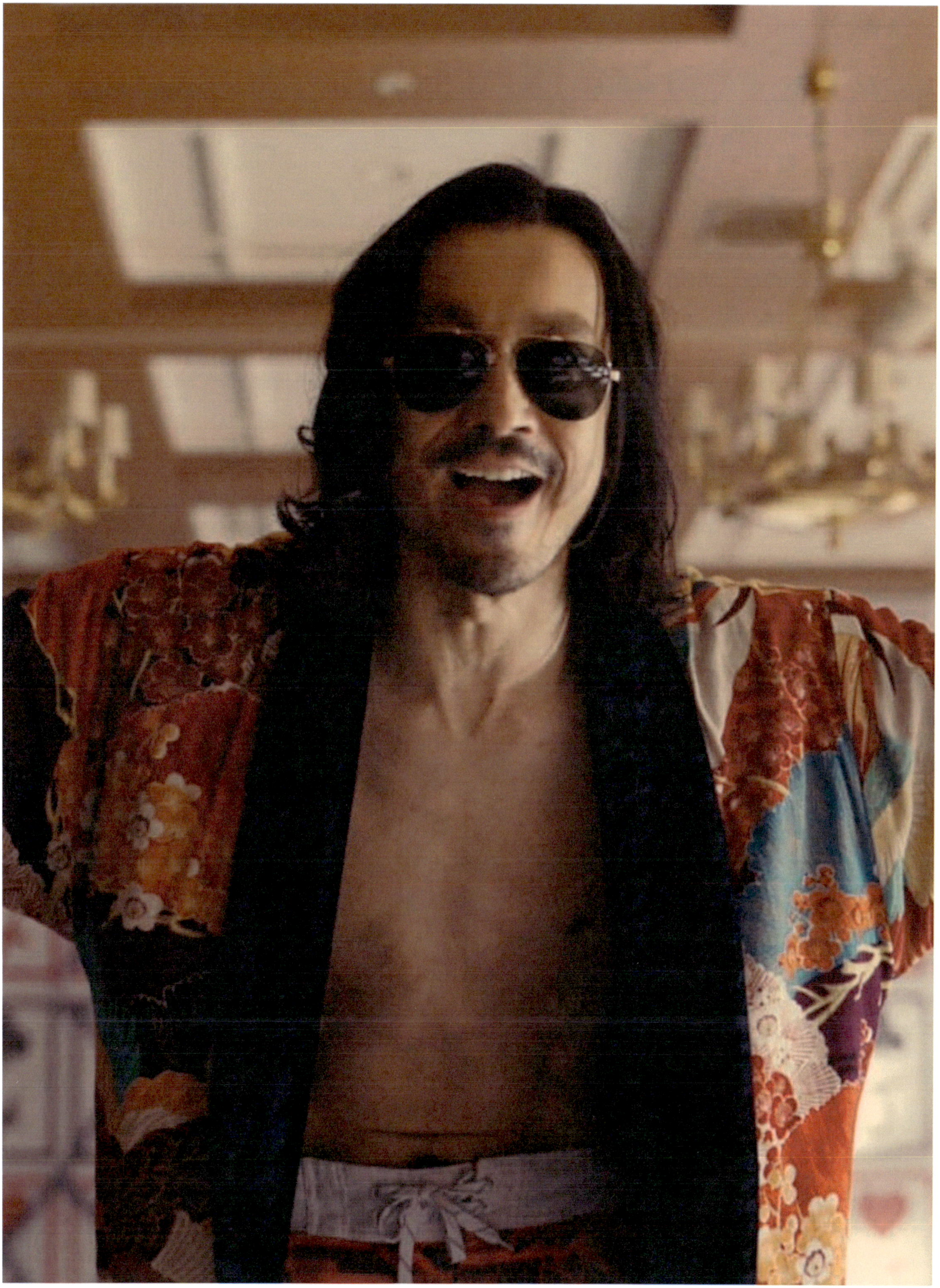

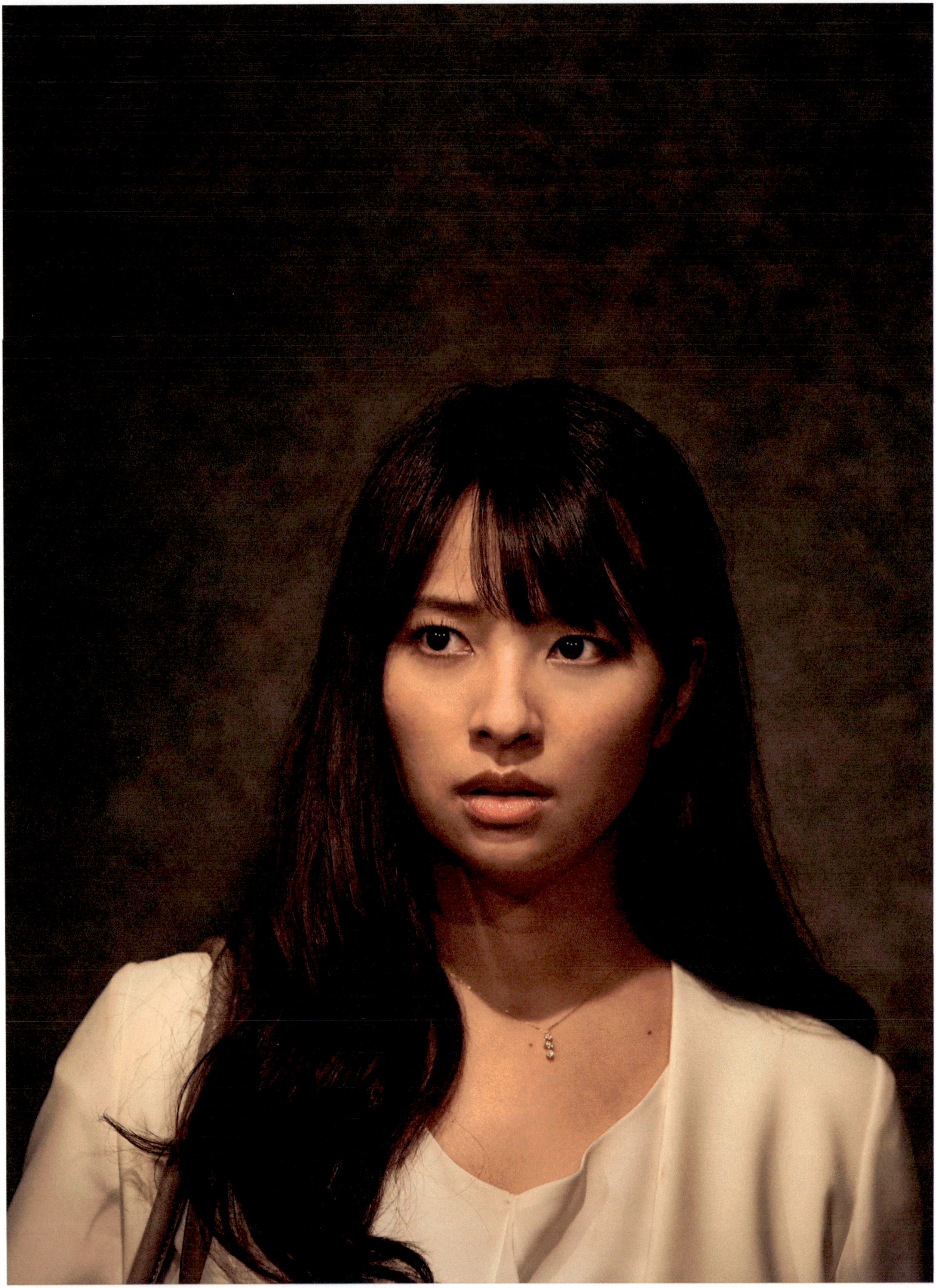

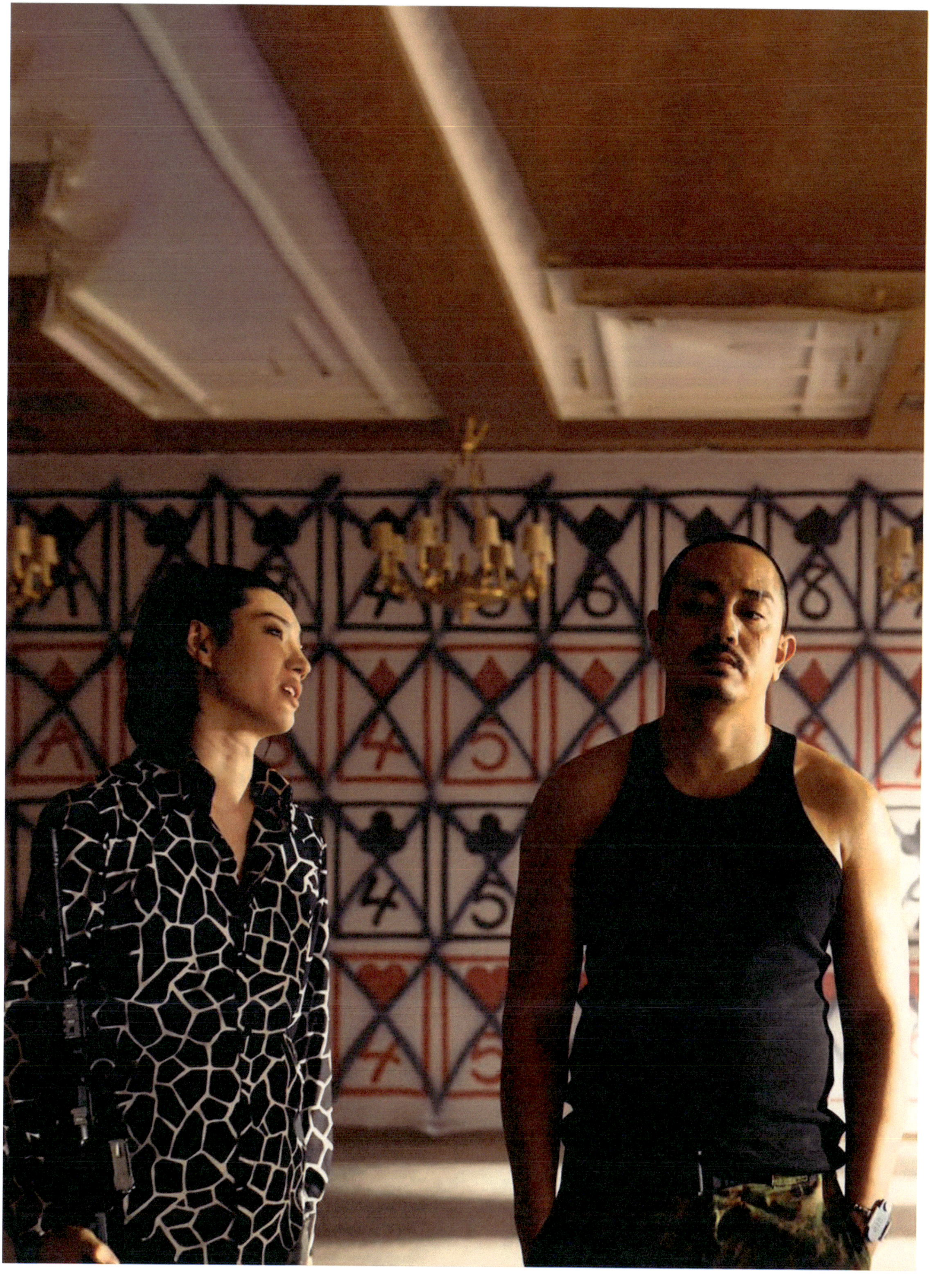

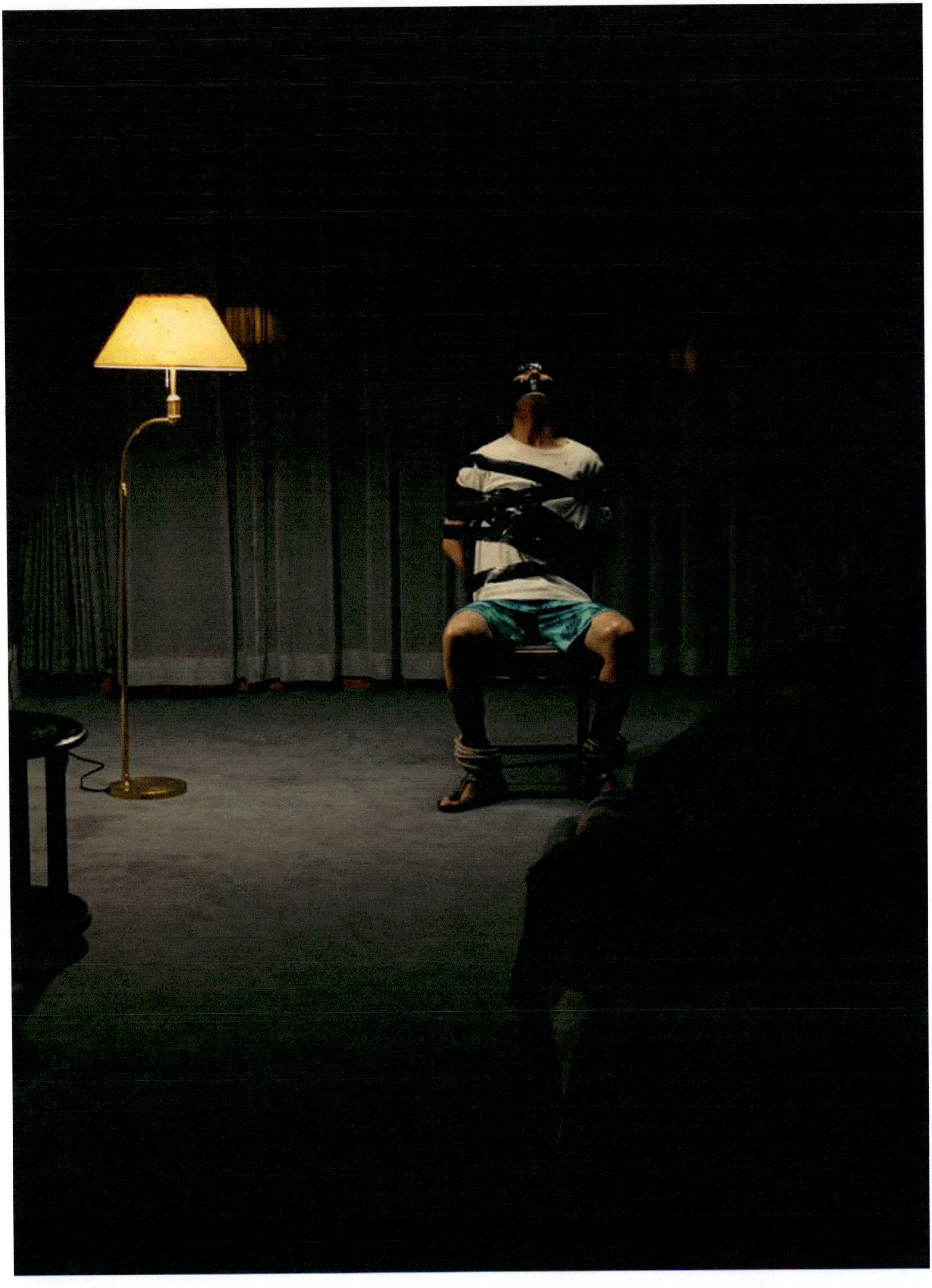

Made in the USA
Columbia, SC
02 March 2025

54577864R00024